Overcoming
Bias

Berrett-Koehler Publishers, Inc.

1333 Broadway, Suite 1000, Oakland, CA 94612-1921
Tel: (510) 817-2277   Fax: (510) 817-2278   www.bkconnection.com

Ordering Information

Quantity sales. Special discounts are available on quantity purchases by corporations, associations, and others. For details, contact the "Special Sales Department" at the Berrett-Koehler address above.

Individual sales. Berrett-Koehler publications are available through most bookstores. They can also be ordered directly from Berrett-Koehler: Tel: (800) 929-2929; Fax: (802) 864-7626; www.bkconnection.com

Orders for college textbook/course adoption use. Please contact Berrett-Koehler: Tel: (800) 929-2929; Fax: (802) 864-7626.

Orders by U.S. trade bookstores and wholesalers. Please contact Ingram Publisher Services, Tel: (800) 509-4887; Fax: (800) 838-1149; E-mail: customer.service@ingram-publisherservices.com; or visit www.ingrampublisherservices.com/Ordering for details about electronic ordering.

Berrett-Koehler and the BK logo are registered trademarks of Berrett-Koehler Publishers, Inc.

Printed in the United States of America

Berrett-Koehler books are printed on long-lasting acid-free paper. When it is available, we choose paper that has been manufactured by environmentally responsible processes. These may include using trees grown in sustainable forests, incorporating recycled paper, minimizing chlorine in bleaching, or recycling the energy produced at the paper mill.

Library of Congress Cataloging-in-Publication Data

Names: Jana, Tiffany, author. | Freeman, Matthew, author.
Title: Overcoming bias : building authentic relationships across differences
    / Tiffany Jana and Matthew Freeman.
Description: First Edition. | Oakland, CA : Berrett-Koehler Publishers, 2016. |
    Includes bibliographical references.
Identifiers: LCCN 2016029693 | ISBN 9781626567252 (pbk.)
Subjects: LCSH: Prejudices. | Stereotypes (Social psychology) | Interpersonal
    relationships.
Classification: LCC BF575.P9 J35 2016 | DDC 305--dc23
LC record available at https://lccn.loc.gov/2016029693

First Edition

21 20 19 18 17 16   10 9 8 7 6 5 4 3 2 1

Interior design and production: Dovetail Publishing Services
Cover designer: Dan Tesser / Studio Carnelian

Overcoming
Bias

Building authentic relationships
across differences

Tiffany Jana ◆ Matthew Freeman

BK

Berrett–Koehler Publishers, Inc.
a BK Life book

To our parents, without whom we may have been too biased to fall in love across differences.

Contents

Preface

Overcoming bias: building authentic relationships across differences is about our human tendency to prefer some things and people more than others, and how to be intentional about not mistrusting people who are different from us. Bias, simply put, is the preference for one thing over another. Preferring warm weather over cold weather is a bias. Bias is a survival instinct that helps the human brain make rapid choices in a world where we are bombarded by thousands of choices every day. The problem with bias is that it doesn't stop at *weather*; it extends to rapid choices about which groups of people we instinctively trust and which we mistrust or fear.

We use the word "differences" in the title and throughout the book because without differences there would be no bias, particularly toward or against people. It's easy to get along with people who are like us. When people share similar values, perspectives, and experiences, we can relate to them. What's challenging is when we want or need to build relationships with people from different walks of life.

Differences can be about anything from educational background to age. Differences also include such hotly politicized topics as race, religion, and immigration status. Differences are not limited to any of these areas and can include anything that is different from you, the reader. Those are the only differences that matter as you use this book, because they are the ones that will challenge you. And yes, this is a book you use. You don't just read it. The book includes exercises and activities designed to help you navigate bias and increase your fluency on the subject.

If we do not choose to overcome our biases, we can inadvertently harm relationships and alienate people with our thoughtless autopilot responses. And collectively, these individual biases create disparate outcomes in our institutions, from education to health care to workplaces. Most often, we harbor biases that we have simply failed to reconsider as we have matured and gained more experience. We can consciously hold one set of beliefs while we unconsciously hold onto misguided ideas we encountered in our youth but never *reexamined*. This book will help you or someone you know clean out those cobwebs and build stronger, more authentic relationships—across difference.

We wrote this book because we work in management consulting, where we are constantly faced with challenges that emerge as a result of unchecked bias. We see everything from employees who feel unheard and undervalued to those who feel their only recourse is to file discrimination or harassment lawsuits.

We wrote this for individuals who want to take control of the bias conversation, understand it better, and take action to help themselves or the people around them. There is no need to wait until employees become disengaged or, worse, until someone sues you or your company. On a personal level, you don't have to stand idly by and let your trusted friend or your crazy uncle say biased things that you know cause harm to others. The information in this book can provide you with the skills you, your friends and family, or your teams need to work together and relate to each other with respect and compassion. Our goal is to provide you with everything you need to understand bias, talk about it with increased fluency, and overcome it so you can build stronger relationships in your personal and professional lives.

Introduction

Why is everybody biased but me?

Have you noticed a lot of conversations, articles, and news coverage about bias? Have you questioned yourself and wondered whether you have bias or noticed places where you experience your own bias or someone else's? Are you looking for ways to recognize whether bias is getting in the way of your relationships or your success in the workplace? If so, we can help. Human bias is a fact of life. It is an annoying and frustrating part of life, but we have all been in situations where we see it and think, "Oh no. This is not really happening. How could he think that what he is saying is OK?" Or worse, "Why did I just say that?" Most of us are paralyzed in those situations, not because we are bad people, but often because we don't want to make a bad situation worse.

In this book we discuss why bias matters, we define the terms we believe will increase your fluency on the subject, and we talk about how you can move from thinking about bias to taking meaningful action to overcome it. Bias matters because we all have it and if you leave it unchecked, it can cause you to inadvertently push people away. This is precisely why we talk about building authentic relationships across differences. This book provides the tools you need to build and strengthen relationships without your unconscious biases getting in the way. You will find exercises, games, and activities to help you connect to your thought patterns and become more proactive and less reactive.

So what exactly do we mean when we say "overcoming" bias? By overcoming, we mean to control, conquer, and prevail over your bias. We have already stated and will continue to state that bias is not something you are immune to. Again, we all have it. One way to overcome bias is to control it instead of letting it control you. Think of it as curbing a bad habit, just like, say, smoking or eating too many sweets. You have to learn to control your cravings, which begins by becoming more self-aware about your behavior, what triggers your desire, and experiment with strategies to interrupt your bad habit. Since control starts with awareness, chapter 1 will include some exercises to help you identify your biases. If you do not know what biases you harbor, you are powerless against them and may be harming others unintentionally. In this case, ignorance is not bliss; ignorance is privilege. A lack of awareness of your own bias allows you to move through the world without consideration for the impact your behaviors and attitudes have on others. Privilege is not a dirty word; it is simply something that works in our favor, an advantage of sorts. Taking the time to control your bias by raising your awareness of your bias is the first step in neutralizing privilege. Unchecked privilege can manifest as bias, so taking the inventory we present in chapter 1 is very useful.

You can conquer your biases once you know what they are and accept whatever implications they may have in your life and relationships. Some may balk at the idea that you can actually conquer your bias, but we disagree. Here's what we mean: In any one instance where bias may influence how you treat someone, you can slow yourself down and make rational choices instead of relying on the subconscious parts of your brain. If successful, you will have conquered your bias in that moment. Some of the exercises in this book, like Activity #4: Devil's Advocate and Activity #5: Get Out of the Zone, require you to confront your biases. It will be uncomfortable at times, but who conquers anything without a little apprehension and discomfort? You will read an example of coauthor Tiffany Jana conquering a specific bias against an entire demographic of people. It took building an authentic relationship with someone from that demographic to help her identify and control her bias. Over time, she was able to conquer that particular bias and move on to identifying other areas for self-improvement. She conquered her bias about a whole nation of people when she made them part of her in-group. (You will learn more about that in chapter 3.)

We argue that you can prevail over your bias through sustained, lifelong effort. Think of the difference between conquering and prevailing like this: The United States arguably conquered Iraq when the military deposed Saddam Hussein, but the installation of a democracy has so far been a failure. You might say we conquered Iraq but we did not prevail there. If you take steps to control your bias and conquer it during critical moments, then over time you just may build the reflexes that allow you to prevail over your bias for the long term. Conquering is about winning the battle; prevailing is about winning the war. Using Tiffany's example, identifying the bias was step one—controlling it through raised awareness. Step two was conquering the bias after many successful, authentic interactions with someone across difference that led to a friendship. Step three was prevailing, when she ceased seeing the group to which her new friend belonged as "other." Their differences still existed, but they no longer affected her emotions or behaviors negatively. Prevailing over bias means that unbiased behavior (where there was once a known bias) is an autonomic response, like breathing or your heartbeat. You no longer have to force it into consciousness or make unbiased choices. It becomes the default setting—but only for that specific bias. Then you must move on to the next bias and start the process over again. Or you can apply the same principle on a larger scale to influence systemic bias—large-scale institutional bias.

An authentic relationship is one that is genuine. It lacks an ulterior motive and is reliable and trustworthy. Authentic

3

relationships are established on the premise that each party is of equal value regardless of age, station, color, gender, or any other variable—just two people connecting on the basis of their shared humanity. Relationships can be authentic without being overly intimate. One need not bear one's soul to prove authenticity. Rather, within the appropriate confines of the particular relationship, two people should simply be genuine, present, and without ill intent. Again, boundaries are fine, but an authentic relationship is significant regardless of emotional distance. Once authenticity is established as a baseline, a person's humanity cannot and should not be unseen or devalued. Some of the hallmarks of authentic relationships include curiosity, kindness, care, concern, empathy, compassion, presence, shared values, pride, sincerity, inclusion, warmth, listening, respect, and understanding.

Human relationships are complicated. Coauthor Tiffany Jana remembers being in a taxi and the driver asked about her occupation. "When I said I worked on diversity and inclusion issues, the driver launched into a passionate monologue about black people and how he just didn't understand what all the fuss was about," recalls Jana. The driver was a retired, white male who genuinely meant no harm. He talked about his alcoholic father and how the driver simply made a choice to never live in poverty again. He thought poor black people should likewise choose not to be poor.

How do the taxi driver's words strike you? Would you have said anything? Would your response depend on who else heard his comments? Often the context of bias is what throws us. Some people feel the need to defend the person or persons on the receiving end of the bias. Other people prefer to avoid conflict if at all possible. Maybe you don't experience the driver's comments as biased at all. There is no single correct response in these situations. You have to do what is comfortable for you.

One of the goals of this book is to help you increase your bias fluency so you can become more aware of bias and move beyond it. **Bulleted statements** in bold throughout the book make great talking points when helping someone navigate their bias. The good news is that you are also human and may identify a few tips to navigate your own bias. One of the best ways to influence personal growth in others is to show them your own. For this reason we will reveal personal accounts of our own bias and our attempts to overcome it. We will also introduce you to many other people who have confronted their biases and, in turn, helped their friends and colleagues do the same.

We would not be writing this book if we didn't believe that people could overcome bias. We have met hundreds of people who are comfortable claiming their bias and discussing how they move past it. You will meet some of those good people as we share their stories in the chapters that follow. We share our own stories, as well. We have had to take a long hard look at our own biases in order to really be effective at helping others. And our most basic advice is this: build authentic relationships across difference. What kind of difference? All kinds! Race, religion, nationality, and sexual orientation are the human differences that dominate the news, but in reality all human differences can create division, from personality, to generation, to what sports you watch. The most problematic biases are those related to differences outside of an individual's control. There's no better way to uncover, challenge, and ultimately overcome these biases, than establishing friendships with real people.

No one expects to get on a bike and just ride effortlessly without ever taking a tumble and scraping a knee. Overcoming bias is no different. We can provide the tools and skills, but be gentle with yourself as you road test these activities. No one becomes a cultural ally overnight, but your intention does matter, and putting yourself out there in service of building authentic relationships across differences is definitely worth it. The really good news is that as more of us accept our individual responsibility for owning our biases and overcoming them, the potential impact on systemic bias is significant. Systemic bias is the large-scale bias of systems and institutions that perpetuate disparities and unequal outcomes that favor some groups over others. Those disparities decrease social mobility and divide people within nations. They affect health, wealth, and every social wellness indicator measured by economists around the globe. This is an international phenomenon, not only an American one. We see leaders grappling with bias issues when we consult internationally. Systemic bias has been baked into institutions around the world, and although the current generation in power did not create it, we are complicit if we fail to dismantle bias by starting with our own.

Now, we do have to warn you that if overcoming bias were easy, this introduction would be the end of the book. But it is not easy, which is why we've written this book. It will provide you with the tools and skills to make talking about and overcoming bias easier. When you finish this book, if you notice your own bias, or find yourself listening to someone else's bias, you will be better equipped as a cultural ally who can stand up and address the bias intelligently, compassionately, and effectively.

Chapter One

If you're a man, or you have men in your life, here's some news you can use: grow a beard. Seriously. Men with beards are seen as more trustworthy. Two men advertising the same product, one with a beard and one without, make customers feel differently. The fact is, bearded salesmen sell more stuff.[1] Most people would tell you beards on spokesmen don't sway them, but they'd be wrong. Why? Because our brains have subtle preferences that we don't even know about. Americans, it turns out, have a pro-beard bias.

As a cultural ally, someone who seeks to expand their understanding of others and use it for good, you probably have a sense of what bias is. Many people know it when they see it, but can't define it very well. Here is a simple definition to prevent any confusion:

- **Bias is the tendency to favor one thing over another.**

What types of things might a person favor over another? Well, anything really—a person might prefer certain flavors, colors, textures, sports, cities, teams, etc. No one really gets bent out of shape over flavor bias. Tiffany, for example, can't stand spicy flavors.

> *I just don't like them. Spicy food hurts, it burns and stings, and I do not find eating it a pleasant experience at all. When I try to go with the flow and enjoy spicy*

food like all of the happy spice eaters around me, I feel like I am entering some sort of twisted endurance challenge. Will my bias against spicy food ever make front-page news? Probably not. Will it ever ruin a relationship? Not likely, but it could cause some strain depending on how aggressively I choose to pursue my sweeter, more bland taste. But you get the idea.

● Bias is a natural, normal human tendency.

People are only biased because that is how we are hardwired. The scientists who study human behavior believe that bias exists as a human survival mechanism. If our brains could not, within a split second, tell the difference between an angry lion and a harmless gazelle, we would not have lasted long as a species. And so our brain has evolved to make snap decisions based on making sense of what we see in the blink of an eye. So please don't judge your biased friends, family, or colleagues too harshly. The people around you are human and are designed to have bias. Our job as cultural allies is to find whatever opportunities we can to help people see their bias (because no one really wants to name or claim their bias).

● Most bias is harmless.

So here is the rub. We don't care about each other's favorite color or bias toward a particular travel destination. But you have already guessed it: The bias minefield is wherever someone has a bias about people. If you want to see all hell break loose, express bias about a person or group of people who share some sort of similarity. Depending upon who is listening, you can get yourself in all sorts of trouble. Interpersonal or intergroup bias is exactly what makes headlines. Expressing bias toward or against people and acting on that bias gets people fired.

● *It is really hard to acknowledge personal bias.*

That, too, is not anyone's fault. OK, maybe we can blame that on society at large. Who the heck wants to stand up and say, "Hey, look over here! I am totally biased against _____." (Fill in the blank with something about people, then duck as the arrows come flying toward you.) We have made it dangerous for people to tell the truth about their thoughts, whether conscious or subconscious. In our highly politicized society, people have even taken heat for acknowledging *past* biases. In 2010, Shirley Sherrod was fired from her position with the Department of Agriculture after a politically conservative blog selectively edited a speech of hers to make it sound as if she was biased against white people. In fact, she had done the admirable task of acknowledging that traumatic childhood experiences with white people had influenced her in ways that she became aware of and uncomfortable with. She was telling her story of overcoming bias—which was selectively edited and used to get her fired. The Obama administration apologized and offered her a job, which she ultimately declined. Nevertheless, her story demonstrates how hard it is to acknowledge even a former bias you have worked hard to set aside.

So if and when someone near you lets some bias show, let's have a little compassion and see if we can help them, not hurt them. If you want to have a little fun and test yourself and your friends for bias, here is an easy activity for you. Just remember, everyone has bias. So don't feel bad when you discover your own biases, and tell your friends not to beat themselves up about it when they do as well. Acknowledging it is the first step.

Activity #1 – Job Association

Your brain catalogs information to help you make snap judgments. Previous experiences, lessons from your family, messages gleaned from the media—all this and more inform how you navigate the world. If you want to know how this works, try this exercise. Fill in the first word or phrase that comes to mind when you see the following job titles.

Used car salesman: _____

Politician: _____

Lawyer: _____

Teacher: _____

Doctor: _____

Activity #1 often elicits stereotypes that people have about the professions listed. Unfortunately, this tendency to stereotype does not stop when we move beyond career choices. If we were to repeat the same exercise with racial, ethnic, gender, or sexual orientation groups, the associations would come just as easily.

● **Stereotypes lead to bias if you believe them.**

Stereotypes assume that people who share one characteristic, such as sex or skin color, share all other traits. We all know some: blondes are airheaded, men are aggressive, Americans don't know anything about other countries. This does not mean that there isn't any truth to stereotypes; they just can't be applied to everyone in the group. One of our favorite examples of this is the fact that Fortune 500 CEOs are taller than the average population. It's true. Look it up. So why are they taller? Well, studies suggest that Fortune 500 CEOs are taller than average because people have a positive bias toward tall people. Height is often associated with power and leadership, so at some point American society stereo-typed tall people as better leaders.

A more common stereotype is that Asian people are good at math. We are quite certain that many are good at math. A lot of other people are good at math, too. We are also confident that plenty of Asian people are not good at math. But still, the common stereotype might affect the outcome of a job interview without the hiring manager even realizing it. These stereotypical ideas are often locked deep in the recesses of our minds just waiting to creep up and get in the way of our better judgment, fueling the bias—or automatic preferences—we have for one group over another.

● *If you aren't aware of the stereotypes you believe, you can't overcome them.*

This kind of unconscious bias is certainly relevant to the politically hot topics of race, gender, and sexual orientation. And evidence shows how our brains lead us to make irrational decisions based on a number of factors. A few examples:

- ♦ Men with beards are considered more trustworthy than clean-shaven men.

- ♦ People with accents that are foreign to us are trusted less than people with accents similar to our own.

- ♦ More people die in female-named hurricanes than in male-named hurricanes, perhaps because people think female names represent less of a threat.

- ♦ A hiring manager who's holding a warm drink in his or her hand is more likely to hire a job candidate than when interviewing a similar candidate while holding a cold drink.

Activity #1 helps identify unconscious biases. Activity #2 measures different kinds and intensities of bias. Maybe we should have named this book Having Fun with Bias since there are so many games in here! Some people find this topic depressing and intimidating, but you can have fun with it. In fact, if you are planning to intervene and help some of your well-meaning associates dial down their bias, fun is actually a great approach.

Activity #2 – Implicit Association Test

For this exercise you'll need to take the Project Implicit Implicit Association Test (IAT). To take the test, visit

https://implicit.harvard.edu/implicit

and take the online. The IAT, hosted at Harvard University, allows you to test yourself for over a dozen different biases, including those involving race, skin tone, weight, age, and disability. Even if you are certain you don't have any bias, take Harvard's test and see how you score. Don't worry, they don't know who you are and no one will know your scores unless you tell them. Project Implicit does collect general demographic information like age and gender, because it's a study and they are collecting data. No names or contact information are required.

Most people try to behave decently and not be racist or sexist. Nevertheless, our brains don't break the habit of categorizing things when we see people. And so, despite our best intentions, we generalize and rely on mental shortcuts when we deal with people. What thoughtful person wants to determine someone else's worth based on the color of her skin? Or make promotional decisions because of a candidate's height? Clearly these criteria are absurd—and yet, we rely on them every day, without even realizing it.

● **Bias can get in the way of our personal goals and intentions.**

We assume that if you're reading this book, you believe in equality and trying to treat people fairly. If so, then you need to know your brain can get in the way. If equality and fairness don't motivate you, perhaps success and advancement do. Overcoming your bias can help you build better relationships, and those relationships can pave your path to advancement in your career and in life. Thank goodness science is advancing at such a fast pace. If you have a particularly skeptical friend or someone who won't take anyone but an expert's word for it, refer her or him to the research we've listed in the back of this book.

You have probably noticed all the talk about bias, race, gender, sexual orientation, and the like in the news. Clearly the world is paying attention to the new science and to people's concerns about how they are being treated. This is a good thing. So why isn't that enough?

● **Bias can give us blind spots that make it harder to see someone else's point of view.**

Despite the best intentions to treat everyone fairly, bias can give us enormous blind spots. Those blind spots make us unable to see things from another person's point of view. And when people act on their biases, it creates a downward spiral, where the victims of bias trust others even less. People who are on their guard don't tend to make friends easily or be particularly warm and fuzzy.

A friend of ours remembers a cross being burned on her family's property and has painful associations with the Confederate battle flag because the people who did it were open Confederate sympathizers. It is a challenge, given her family history, to trust any fliers of or apologists for that flag. And when she sees someone with a Confederate battle flag sticker on his car, what do you think she feels?

On the other hand, many who fly the Confederate battle flag don't know or don't care how it has been used as a symbol of racial terrorism, preferring to focus on their ancestors' wartime sacrifices. And in this way, disconnection and division are sowed and reaped within our society, as two groups with very different experiences of the same symbol cannot or will not understand each other.

● Bias can be passed from generation to generation.

The origins of many biases are not a mystery. People are social animals—we depend on the herd for survival. But who is part of our herd? Who is safe, trustworthy? Who will take care of us, and who will hurt us? As babies, our brains memorize the look of the faces around us and think of those that are similar looking as safe for the rest of our lives. What happens when we see people who look different from what we saw growing up? Features that we did not see in childhood register in a different part of the brain, a part more associated with the emotion of fear. Being members of a herd, a tribe, or a group—what we call an "in-group" is hardwired into our brains (see chapter 3). It is essential to our survival as a species. The good news is that our definition of in-group can change. Throughout the rest of this book we will talk about how to shake up the mix of nature and nurture that makes it hard for us to trust people outside of our clan.

Beyond what we see, what we experience also shapes who we become and what we believe. Even our trusted friends' and family's personal experiences and biases shape our own biases. In other words, we learned from mom and dad (or who raised us) what kinds of people are trustworthy.

People often hope that the next generation will fix all of the bias-related failures of the previous generations. This is where the playground example comes in. Small children play on the playground with other children without regard for race, color, gender, religion, and so on. Unfortunately, playground politics don't last. Eventually children notice cues from parents and peers—for example, mom clutching her purse and scurrying the child along when someone suspicious walks too close. Children are programmed to pay attention to these cues. Sometimes the messages are overt—"You are not allowed to play with kids from THAT school"—or there is subtle social pressure from a popular peer to avoid or mistreat certain people. When those overt and subtle messages form a pattern of biased treatment toward or against a specific group—people with disabilities, or a race, sex, or class— biased leanings take root in young minds and follow them through adulthood. The biased people you know often learned their bias from people who raised or mentored them. Sometimes you can help people whose bias slips out just by asking them *why* they believe what they believe about a person or group of people. You may get a perfectly sensible response. These folks may also dig a deeper and deeper hole with every word as they try to rationalize an irrational bias. Do not laugh. Do not judge. Just listen. You may learn valuable information that can help you help them.

Think about it. Can you recall your parents' or guardians' biases? How did their opinions and experiences shape yours? We have a good friend named Manny, born in the 1940s, who recalls his mother locking the car doors when they crossed into the Dakotas on their family road trip. He said, "Mom, why are we locking the doors?" She replied, "Indians. This place is crawling with Indians." Such parental bias is a strong influence regardless of the decade. And every generation harbors cultural fears. Manny thought the Indians were hiding around the corner to get them. He ultimately became a skilled diversity practitioner and, in doing so, examined his own biases and early influences. We heard this story when Manny, an older white male, shared it in front of dozens of people during diversity training. He used his experience to show that well-meaning people inadvertently share their misperceptions with others, including, and especially, their children. Manny thought Native Americans were to be feared because he received bad information. It is vitally important that we help our friends, family, and colleagues consider the biases they have and the source from which they originated. Does time, context, or a change in personal perspective affect what they believe over time? We think it does, but people don't stop often enough to take an inventory of what they believe and why they believe it.

Tiffany was born in El Paso, Texas, and has this to say:

As a result of my proximity to the border with Mexico, many of my friends, doctors, teachers, and babysitters were Mexican. I also spoke Spanish before I spoke English due to my access to the Mexican border and Mexican people. The early influences of Mexican culture on my life made an indelible impression on my worldview. I am sitting in a café in Texas, visiting for the first time in 30 years, and everything about the place makes me nostalgic for my childhood. The southwestern art, the Mexican cultural references, and the majority Spanish-speaking population warms my soul. I have a positive bias toward Mexico, Mexicans, and Spanish-speaking people because I associate all of it with my childhood. I happen to have had an unusually wonderful childhood.

But even a positive bias can create problems. I, unfortunately, have a known irrational response when one of my biases is triggered. The tone of the immigration debate infuriates me, particularly when people express negative stereotypes about Mexican people. The minute I hear people talking negatively about the people I consider family by association, I feel the heat rise in my face. My speech quickens, my blood boils, and I am at the ready with a dozen comebacks, many of which I would probably not use in a rational conversation where my emotions had not been piqued. Say something bad about Mexicans and you may as well insult my mother. That is funny, because I am not aware of any Mexican ancestry in my family.

Bias works both ways. It can influence your opinion toward or against people, places, things, and ideas. I have a bias that favors Mexicans.

Our friend Manny had a bias against Native Americans until he learned better. The people who harbor negative stereotypes about Mexicans have negative biases. Why does your bias or mine matter? It matters because when we are confronted with the object of our biases, it can influence our behavior in ways that defy our values and our conscious thought. As Tiffany explains, "I have to fight to think well of a person who says what I consider to be hateful things about Mexican people." They may have experiences that validate their opinions, and their opinions are exactly that—*opinions*. If Manny had met a Native American when he was 12 years old, he would have likely been terrified because he held the opinion that they were inherently dangerous. Had his perspective never been examined, would he have hired an

17

American Indian attorney when he needed one? Would he judge someone of Native ancestry more harshly when her character was called into question? When we harbor unconscious biases, they can wreak havoc on our better judgment.

● *Bias is in the air you breathe.*

You could have the most inclusive families in the world, however, and still absorb biased information about others. One well-known study analyzed a wide swath of written material—from books to magazines to newspapers—and created a database that approximates what a college-bound student will have read by the time she enters college.[2] It then analyzed how often words were paired in order to understand where stereotyped messages about people might come from.

The study found, perhaps not surprisingly, that we are immersed in a culture that creates and reinforces problematic associations. Black is most commonly paired with the adjectives "poor" and "violent," while white is paired with "wealthy" and "progressive." Males are described most often as "dominant" and "leader," while female pairs most often with "distant" and "warm," perhaps indicating that we assess women for their emotional tone while we expect men to assume leadership positions.

● *Positive bias can be just as harmful as a negative bias.*

Don't think that just because you like something or someone that bias must be a good thing. You will get that response from people you are trying to influence with the ideas in this book. The problem with positive bias is that it can unfairly influence a person's decisions and attitudes against someone else. Positive bias can still fuel exclusion. Positive bias pushes us toward one thing and away from another. That can leave people feeling included or excluded depending on which side of the bias they are on.

CALL TO ACTION

For 24 hours, pay attention to what you see and hear in the media. Try to identify any bias in the perspectives shared.

Chapter Two

So we warned you in the introduction that you should examine your own bias before extending your counsel to others. The best way to teach is to model change. How can we insist that others do the hard work of holding themselves accountable for their biased attitudes and behavior if we have not truly taken the time to closely examine and overcome our own bias? We are going to teach the teacher. Then you can go out and teach the world. We promise, it won't hurt.

So, the process of overcoming your bias starts with you. By overcoming, we mean to control, conquer, and prevail over your bias. With self-awareness, attention, and effort, you can become aware of the way in which bias operates in your life. Then, you can make deliberate choices to minimize the impact your brain's automatic preferences have on how you treat people. Will your brain ever stop having automatic preferences? No. Bias is a hard-wired survival mechanism. Can you ever completely rewire your brain to overwrite its current biases? Maybe—the jury is still out.[1] But what we do know is that you don't have to let your unconscious biases go unchallenged. You can overcome the impact they have on your life.

You are the solution. You are not the cause of the problem. (Feel free to blame society, history, your brain's wiring, and a misguided humanity for creating this mess.) Fortunately, we have more knowledge about the science of the human brain now, and we have the tools to change our thoughts and behaviors. So, get ready to take a long, hard look at yourself.

It begins with breaking the bias cycle. In our work as diversity practitioners and organizational development specialists, we frequently encounter both leaders and individual contributors who wholeheartedly believe that if we could just fix someone else, someone who is not *me*, everything would improve. As human beings, we are often quick to assign blame and situate problems within everyone but ourselves. Hopefully by now you have already taken the Implicit Association Test (see Activity #2) and identified a few of your own biases. If not, don't worry—you still have time. Go ahead, we will wait.

Most people who take the IAT are shocked at the results, but they shouldn't be. We all have bias. We really cannot emphasize that enough. That said, you must realize that it is critically important to acknowledge that you, too, have bias. No one is served by blaming others without self-reflection and awareness of our own issues. We cannot tell you how many times our clients have said, "If only [insert person or group of people] would change, everything would be fine." If we cannot see how we are each a part of the ubiquitous *they*, then we have no hope of change. No one is off the hook when it comes to bias. We all have it and it shows up at some point. We don't have to be victims of our unconscious bias. Most of us don't want to be biased, so we need to learn to control the bias so that our rational, compassionate selves can make better decisions.

Unconscious bias shows up in many forms:

- Crossing the street to avoid certain kinds of people
- Dismissing a qualified job candidate with a foreign accent
- Asking a person of Asian descent where they're *really* from
- Clutching your purse when passing by a black man
- Recommending a man for a promotion from a pool that includes equally qualified women employees

How do you notice your own bias? Start paying attention to how you treat people. Ask yourself, without judgment, if you would make the same choice if the person in front of you were different. Use your imagination: Replace the job candidate with your mother (assuming she had the same résumé as the candidate!). Would you ask the same questions? Would you feel more or less at ease? Replace the pedestrian you pass on the street with your brother. If your brother were wearing the same outfit, would you have crossed the street? Don't neglect personal safety, but do start questioning why your brain believes that one person is trustworthy while another is not. It isn't a comfortable exercise, but it is key to reprogramming your brain.

Honestly, the hardest part of this task is the acknowledgment that you even have bias. Many of us pride ourselves on being ethical, fair, kind, and respectful to all people. However, the results from the thousands of people who have taken the IAT tell a different story. The researchers at Project Implicit have created a test that is widely acknowledged to be an accurate measure of your brain's automatic preference for one of two different choices in a social group, for example: weight (fat or thin), race (black or white), age (young or old), and so forth. You are instructed to tap a key on your computer's keyboard with your left hand (the letter *e*) and a different key with your right hand (the letter *i*). Then, you go through several rounds of an exercise where a social group (e.g., blacks and whites; fat and thin people) is assigned a key, and an evaluative word (e.g., good or bad) is also assigned a key. So, for example, in one round, you are told to hit *e* when you see a picture of a black person and *i* when you see a picture of a white person. When you see a word that is good (e.g., happy) you hit the *e* key, and when you see a word that is bad (e.g., grief) you hit the *i* key. Then you are asked to select which image you associate with each word.

According to the project's website, "The Implicit Association Test measures the strength of associations between concepts (e.g., black people, gay people) and evaluations (e.g., good, bad) or stereotypes (e.g., athletic, clumsy). The main idea is that making a response is easier when closely related items share the same response key. We would say that one has an implicit preference for straight people relative to gay people if they are faster to categorize words when Gay People and Bad share a response relative to when Gay People and Good share a response key."

Based on feedback from the millions of people who have taken the IAT, on the black and white test, the vast majority of folks show an automatic preference for white people.

Very few people showed an automatic preference for black people. Again, according to the Project Implicit website, "Results from this website consistently show that members of stigmatized groups (black people, gay people, older people) tend to have more positive implicit attitudes toward their groups than do people who are not in the group, but that there is still a moderate preference for the more socially valued group. So gay people tend to show an implicit preference for straight people relative to gay people, but it is not as strong as the implicit preference shown by straight people. We think that this is because stigmatized group members develop negative associations about their group from their cultural environments, but also have some positive associations because of their own group membership and that of close others."

For those of you doing the math, the remaining numbers to get to 100 percent were the 17 percent of people who showed no preference for either group.

- **Believing you have no bias is worse than knowing you do.**

Once we can acknowledge our bias, whether through taking formal tests or simply being brutally honest with ourselves, then and only then can we begin to change it. Telling yourself that you have no bias—that you are one of the good guys who believes in equality—is the best guarantee that you will continue letting your unconscious bias control how you treat people.

Another way your bias may show up is through what we call hot buttons, or triggers. Have you ever had your buttons pushed and reacted without thinking? Where your emotional response gets out in front of a rational one? Where you've thought, usually later, "Wow, I wish I hadn't responded like that"? Your family is often the best at knowing and pushing these buttons. In our experience, siblings may be the most effective at setting you off!

● **Topics that consistently make you angry may be hot-button triggers.**

As an example, Tiffany has come to learn that she is sensitive about the immigration conversation in the United States because people often name Mexicans as part of the problem. In this case, the bias is a positive one toward Mexicans or people of Mexican ancestry, but the emotional reaction Tiffany has when confronted with people who act dismissively toward this group helps her see a positive bias toward Mexicans and a negative one toward those who would restrict immigration. This is important information that can provide clues for where biases might impact our ability to fairly treat people—in either unjustified positive or negative ways. She says:

> *After a substantial amount of reflection about why I respond emotionally to negative opinions about Mexicans, I learned that the immigration conversation requires my full attention. I may not be able to control my defensive emotions, but I have learned to moderate my behavior.*

One of the things I do differently is tell people about my connection to Mexico and why it is important to me. This provides the listener access to part of my story and, by extension, my humanity. This way if we disagree later, we are already one step closer to being authentic with each other. I make the connection as soon as I see that the discussion is headed into my bias zone. This act of pre-empting the topic of Mexico before it goes off course serves as a bit of a disclaimer in case my attempts to control my emotional response fail. At least the listener will know from whence my emotions came.

Sometimes the disclaimer, or the personalization of the issue, causes people to rethink their perspective. If they know early on that a certain angle will upset you, they may tone it down. Unfortunately, some people lack a high degree of empathy and will either fail to notice your concern or will carry on and provoke you quite deliberately.

● Hot-button triggers are often linked to unconscious bias.

So, when you notice yourself getting seriously ticked off, or even mildly agitated, pay close attention to the topic. If you start to see a pattern, you may have a bias issue. This also works with friends and family. If you find yourself the victim of harsh words or on the receiving end of a crappy attitude about the same thing with the same person, over and over again, *they* might have a bias issue. And remember, if the topic is choice of pizza shops, it may not be worth engaging. But if the topic is a certain group of people, or religion, or some equally sensitive issue, be a friend and practice some of the talking points we have presented so far.

TIP: Try this sentence stem if someone says something biased and you want to help him or her see that bias: *"You may not be aware of this, but I am uncomfortable with the way you are talking about that group of people."*

This statement lets your friend off the hook in two ways. First, the underlined portion implies that if she knew better, she would do better. The rest of the sentence focuses on your feelings, as opposed to a direct accusation of her bias. Using "I" statements (in this case, "I am uncomfortable") to help people understand how their behavior is affecting the people around them is a time-tested conflict-resolution tool.

Now here is one of the places where our human tendencies get us into real trouble. Peer pressure is real, and it does not stop just because we are adults. We know it's painful to admit, but how many times have you been in a room with someone who said something racist, sexist, or just plain mean—and you went along with it without speaking up? Depending on the relationship, the power dynamic, the level of respect, or, more selfishly, what we want or need from that person, we unfortunately encourage such bad behavior through our silence. We encourage biased behavior when we say nothing in the face of a hateful comment. We encourage biased behavior when we laugh at a sexist or racist joke. We encourage biased behavior when we either vocally or tacitly egg people on by not holding them accountable to a higher standard. And if someone calls you out, try to remember how hard it is to support someone's de-biasing journey and don't take it personally. It is the behavior they are criticizing, not you.

Speaking of taking things personally, try this activity.

Activity #3 – Personalization

Think about your own hot-button issues. What topics or situations get under your skin? Once you have identified a few issues, visualize what happens to you physically when something or someone sets you off. Do you perspire? Does your speech or heart rate increase? Do you tense up or clench your jaw?

We sometimes refer to this process of self-evaluation as "the appendix syndrome." Addressing bias is not like having your appendix removed—a one-time procedure that is completed and never thought about again. It's more like hygiene—we all have to do maintenance to keep it up.[2] Learning your physical and emotional responses is important because they are nonrational clues that help identify what your biases are. Additionally, an inventory of your physical and emotional responses can help you recover more quickly when you've been triggered. When you're aware that you, for example, clench your jaw when your buttons have been pushed, you can sometimes recognize that physical tell before you even recognize the anger and enter more quickly into productive conversations that aren't being dictated by the emotional part of your brain that your bias has activated. Most often, people have hot-button responses because they associate their current situation with some negative past experience. What happens in the moment tends not to be as big a deal as we think it is; rather it's the memory of something else that is triggered.

Now that you have identified a few hot-button issues and your associated physical and emotional responses, find someone in your circle of trust. Ask this person to help you navigate your bias around one of the hot-button topics by having a provocative conversation with you. Your job is to keep your cool, breathe, and figure out how to manage your physical responses. Depending on the intensity of the issue, you may need to allow the topic to show up in your life without your prompting. Don't go looking for trouble if you don't feel ready to manage your triggers. Instead, excuse yourself to take some deep breaths or a short walk when the hot buttons are triggered. Do this until you've gained some familiarity with your physiological "tells" and have developed control over your subsequent responses. This is why practicing with a trusted friend or family member is a safe place to start. This is how you begin to gain control of your bias.

If you were really uncomfortable with that exercise or the thought of it, we've got bad news. Overcoming bias is hard work, and it's not always comfortable. Things that are worthwhile usually take effort, but the payoff is awesome. Learning to ride a bike, swim, read, do your taxes—those all had an uncomfortable learning curve. Setting aside your bias so that you can have authentic interactions with people is worthwhile, but it will take effort if you are not already practiced at it.

So to review, your self-awareness tools are:

1. Take the Implicit Association Test.

2. Practice noticing your biases at work and in everyday life.

3. Identify your hot-button issues.

4. Practice having a calm conversation about your hot-button issues with a trusted friend.

Through these simple steps, you will begin noticing how the unconscious parts of your brain shape your behavior on a regular basis.

Self-awareness about your bias is only the starting point. In order to build relationships across differences, there are other skills and tools you will need.

For starters, you can't build authentic relationships across differences if you never interact with people who are different from you. And what kind of differences matter? Frankly, all kinds. But we are especially interested in this book in helping people build bridges across the divides that were created by societal hierarchies: legally sanctioned racial discrimination, marginalization of women as second-class citizens, ongoing legal discrimination of LGBT people, calls for Muslims or Latinos to be banned from entering the United States. These are examples of divides that had or still have the full legal force of society behind them and have created ongoing disparities in treatment in the judicial system, health outcomes, wealth accumulation, and access to fair housing in healthy neighborhoods.

Simply interacting across differences is not enough, however. Ordering your daily coffee from a woman in a hijab doesn't quite qualify as an authentic relationship with a Muslim. Nor does your childhood relationship with a housekeeper from another country equate to a relationship between equals. It's not that these relationships can't be meaningful or important, but they aren't the kind of relationships that will help you overcome the kinds of biases our society surrounds us with.

● **The skills you need to overcome bias can be taught, learned, and mastered.**

What would you say if we told you that overcoming bias is possible because researchers have outlined and tested a comprehensive theory that tells us it can be done? In fact, it was written about in 1954 and is called contact theory. But at that time, maybe people were not ready to overcome personal and societal bias, because the research has been long neglected.[3] The good news is that the skills and tools required to help people navigate differences and overcome bias are exactly that—skills. Skills to overcome bias can be taught, learned, practiced, and mastered. More good news—reading this book is a great step along the path of mastering the skills to build authentic relationships across difference. The challenging part is that such mastery requires commitment and effort. And let's face it: if the whole world wasn't ready to overcome bias decades ago, it should be no surprise that we still have stragglers. We are glad that you are taking the time to increase your bias fluency so you can help both yourself and others see that it can be done with patience and persistence.

Contact theory is the idea that people can reduce personal bias through cross-cultural experiences.[4] The germinal theorist Gordon Allport hypothesized that prejudice emerges from a lack of understanding of and exposure to different people. It is rooted in our societal segregation. According to contact theory, exposure to different types of people decreases prejudice.[5] What is absolutely crucial in his findings is the following:

● *Simply putting different kinds of people together does not reduce bias.*

Merely being in the same room, the same office, or the same neighborhood with different kinds of people does not reduce interpersonal bias. It turns out five conditions are necessary to overcome bias. We might call these the prerequisites for authenticity in relationships:[6]

---

1. All group members have equal status.
2. Opportunities for meaningful personal encounters are available.
3. Participants are interdependent and working toward a common goal.
4. Stereotypes are actively disconfirmed.
5. The group actively supports equality.

So contact theory sounds great, but what does that practical application look like? In the workplace, we can easily imagine scenarios where we are on teams with different kinds of people working toward a common goal. Working toward that shared goal will, over time, reduce your interpersonal bias. This is a much easier endeavor for individual contributors than it is for managers and supervisors. Leadership positions create inherent inequality unless you are in a group of leadership peers.

This whole concept becomes much more challenging outside the workplace, where we have to actively choose to place ourselves in situations that meet the above criteria. You would have to play intramural sports on a diverse team, volunteer with a diverse group of fellow volunteers, or join a community group without being the leader. Situations like these bring us closer to each other and closer to understanding differences in ways that are personal and meaningful. Exposure to counter-stereotypes actively disconfirms the basis for our bias. We, as cultural allies, must choose to recognize bias-reducing opportunities when they present themselves. We need to move our busy excuses out of the way and choose to address the biases that limit our ability to interact with people authentically and equitably.

Tiffany recounts an early experience with bias and contact theory.

One of my earliest jobs was at a high-end designer outlet in New York. The cheapest item available for purchase was usually a $175 belt. Most women left the shop one to two thousand dollars lighter than when they entered. I received commission on my sales in the form of credit toward the ridiculously expensive clothing. Fortunately for me, I was quite good at sales, so I racked up credits and collected a nice designer *wardrobe over the course of a year or so. The only thing I loathed about my job was the hagglers.*

I could not, for the life of me, understand how anyone could work up the gumption to ask me to reduce the price of clothing that was clearly marked with the retail and often the sales price on the tags! Remember, this was a designer outlet *store. Outlet stores tend to discount their merchandise. The women who haggled were consistently of East Indian descent. The experience of explaining why I could not change the clearly labeled prices without compromising my job, over and over again, was exhausting. I began to associate Indian people with the anxiety I felt every time an Indian-looking person walked in my shop. Was she going to demand a discount? Would this be the time I was offered some trinket just tempting enough in exchange for a price cut? The negative association of conflict with a specific demographic followed me and eventually morphed into a generalization of an entire group of people. I don't know when my psyche made the leap from a specific context to feeling that all Indian people were anxiety inducing. Nonetheless, I developed a very specific bias. I painted a group of people with a broad brush.*

It was not until I served on the board of directors for an innovative art gallery that my bias began to subside. I worked side by side with one of the most brilliant, engaging, and kind people I have ever known. My friend Prabir worked tirelessly to help the gallery become an East Coast destination and shape the downtown arts and culture scene in Richmond, Virginia. Five years of working toward the goal of bringing art to a great community alongside someone different from me changed my perspective and openness toward his entire demographic. I have been that perspective-changing person for many people in my lifetime. It was nice to learn that even when you think you are open minded and inclusive, there is always room for improvement.

We are finishing up this chapter in a hotel in Hong Kong, China. Last night, we were at the Temple Street Night Market, ironically given the story Tiffany just shared, haggling for souvenirs to take home to friends and family. Our Hong Kong survival guidebook told us that the locals would not respect us if we accepted the first price they offered. As Americans, it can be excruciatingly uncomfortable to bargain someone down. Every time one of us successfully talked someone down to a great deal, we felt a pang of guilt because a matter of a few bucks for us goes a lot farther for the seller in Hong Kong. Nonetheless, it is the custom. We attempted to gauge the relative value for us and compromised on what seemed fair for both parties. The sellers genuinely seemed to enjoy the exchange and were quite good at it. Despite our discomfort, we attempted to meet the cultural context and challenge our own preconceived notions of how the world is supposed to work.

We were also instructed not to excessively tip taxi drivers in Hong Kong because elderly residents rely on inexpensive transportation and tourists who leave tips drive up the costs for locals. It seems that everything is a matter of perspective. The more contact you have with the world and its diversity, the broader your perspective can be. An expanded perspective can serve you and your friends well when you need to interact authentically across difference. We are certain you have noticed that well-traveled people seem to have a different way of moving through the world and navigating relationships. We do not think it is a coincidence. Our hope is that through some of our experiences and our friends' experiences, you can gain some of the confidence in relating across differences that comes with exposure and cultural fluency. We can point you in the right direction, but you will eventually have to get out there and try it for yourself. Direct contact with people across differences is your very best bet for overcoming bias.

CALL TO ACTION

Accept that you have bias. Practice owning your humanity and humility by acknowledging a bias to someone you trust. (Tell them you are reading a book to help you work on it, but that you are aware it exists.)

Chapter Three

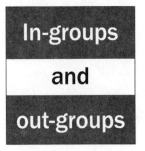

Let's start with some good news: you probably already have the foundation for building authentic relationships across differences. You likely treat people with respect, listen, empathize, and stick with your friends through disagreements and challenging times. We are also fairly certain that your friends, colleagues, and family members do, as well. The problem is not that you and your peers are unfamiliar with healthy behavior. The problem is that you and they, like the rest of us, may be limiting your best behaviors to what we call the "in-group," or the people we know and like best. An in-group might be people who went to the same university you did, people from your hometown, or, more problematically, people who share racial and cultural similarities to you. Remember from the previous chapters that when the bias relates to people-based differences, particularly the ones we cannot change or control, that is where trouble lurks. People who are not part of this in-group, however it's defined, become an out-group. Unfortunately, we tend to demand more from out-groups in order to trust them, or to see them as competent.

● *Differences that people cannot control or change are biases we need to look out for.*

The phenomenon of in-groups and out-groups undercuts efforts to build relationships across difference. When groups are in conflict, explicit pressure can be exerted to prevent cross-group friendships. More often we simply find it easier to hang out with people with whom we can quickly build trust, because they understand our histories, get our jokes, and share our values. Part of your work of building authentic relationships across differences in order to overcome bias is to begin to notice how the in-group and out-group phenomenon works in your own life, and begin to expand your own in-group.

That lack of trust in out-groups is one of the reasons we should look for the similarities even in the face of obvious differences. Every time a hot political topic gains the spotlight in the national or international media, your Facebook feed probably lights up with political commentary. You know you have diversity in your relationships if at least some of the opinions and positions make you crazy. When that happens, most of us question the sanity of our family members or misguided acquaintances. But how often do we stop and engage in conversations that seek to understand an opinion we disagree with—even the politically charged ones? We don't need agreement to be authentic, but we do need respectful, honest communication.

We had the distinct privilege of facilitating a special program for the Congressional Leadership Institute, a partnership between two Washington, DC–based nonprofits, Search for Common Ground and the Faith and Politics Institute. The program was a bipartisan, dialogue-based, 18-month series of conferences with a race and democracy theme. Members of Congress, Democrat and Republican, discussed some of the most challenging topics, and they came together based on the values and goals they had in common. Obviously this is no easy task, but they understood the need and the urgency of working together.

One episode that took place during the conference series offered a poignant illustration of the difficulty of expanding your in-group. The congressional delegation from two different parties went to watch a sports championship game together, and they posted some pictures on Twitter of their bipartisan group cheering for their respective teams. The result? Angry responses from their constituents for collaborating with "the enemy." Democrats sent angry messages to their Democrat representatives, and Republicans did the same. There is tremendous pressure in our society *not* to expand your in-group, so don't make the mistake of thinking it is an easy journey.

Of course not all members of Congress participated in our dialogues, but the ones who did are very forward thinking and built lasting relationships as a result. Can you imagine how much the United States and the world could accomplish if all of our leaders were willing to come together to seek solutions despite the differences that divide them?

● *Honor the differences while seeking similarities.*

Studies of human infants show that people are social animals who display positive bias toward people who look like their immediate family and toward people they are exposed to early in life.[1] Fortunately, however, those positive preferences can change and we can learn to expand our "family." We need people who are willing to overcome their subconscious preferences for people who look, act, and think like they do if we are to truly overcome bias.

Tiffany, for instance, was almost always the only black girl in predominantly white schools and neighborhoods. Her early familial influences were still African American, but her friends were as different from her as you can imagine. She recounts her experience here:

> *The people around me were white, and while that privileged them societally, my parents were doctors, which privileged me socioeconomically. The interesting thing is that when it came time to get married, I had somehow received a cultural cue that people are supposed to marry within their own tribes. How many interracial couples did you know in the 1990s? Even if you*

knew several, how many of them were black women with white or Asian men? Statistically speaking, it is still rare today, but it was even more so back then. So I attempted twice to marry within my tribe, and twice those unions failed. I am not implying that they failed because of race alone, but what I learned was that beyond skin color, I had little in common with my first two husbands. Sometimes you have to rewind the messages of your life and reevaluate their accuracy and relevance.

In this case, Tiffany's bias favored her in-group—people of color. The in-group bias was the default, the assumption. Sometimes, cultural cues and messages are tacit and they become part of people's decision-making matrix unbeknownst to them. What other messages might we be sending and receiving that we are unaware of?

- **Don't be afraid to question your own beliefs and family values.**

Tiffany's upbringing was akin to that of a middle-class white American girl. Nonetheless, the pressure to culturally conform was strong, and she has always marched to the beat of her own drummer.

I believe I had a subconscious preference for the family portraits that had surrounded me my whole life—parents, grandparents, aunts and uncles. Most everyone around me was half of a brown couple. Who was I to break tradition? Well, I finally did and it was a total paradigm shift. I have more in common with my white husband than I did with both of my black husbands combined. And let's not forget that I do race and diversity work for a living, wear dreadlocks, and am quite comfortable and happy being a black woman. This is by no means a denial of identity. It is a recognition that I did not have to submit to a subconscious bias toward my primary in-group in order to find love and compatibility.

● **Be aware of your in-groups, but don't let them control your decisions. You are an individual first.**

In-groups and out-groups are not always clear and consistent. Our friend, journalist and professor Chris Dovi, shared a story of in-groups and out-groups from his own life.

My father's family is Italian, and they're particularly dark complected, with black, very curly hair. As a young kid, I looked to be right out of the mold, minus the curly hair. Growing up in Hampton Roads in the late 1970s and early 1980s, I attended a small Catholic school where the student body was either upper-middle-class, blond-haired, blue-eyed locals, or refugees from South and Central American countries taken in by the Carmelite nuns who ran the school. There was no in between . . . except me.

The two groups did not mix. I found myself stuck in the middle, but excluded by both. Unable to speak Spanish, I was confusing to the Latino students, who wouldn't interact with me. The white students were also confused and didn't tend to associate with me because I looked like the Latino students they were accustomed to looking down on. It was a strange bit of irony that the school also was home to a small group

*of black students, and they were better and more eas-
ily accepted by white students at the school.*

    *You really can't call this treatment racism—eight-
year-olds shouldn't be saddled with a label like that.
But it definitely introduced me to the idea of being
"other," and I carry that experience with me. And I
know that, from their own perspective, these are the
formative experiences that my classmates carry with
them as well, informing their adult ideas that harden
into the -isms that are so much easier to label. I try to
use this experience as a reminder to myself that I must
consider all sides and all experiences when dealing
with people's "natural" prejudices. We all have them.
And while there may be right or wrong ideas—even
though which of these are right or wrong changes with
seasons and generations—there are no right or wrong
people. There are people carrying with them the collective baggage of their life experiences.*

Chris uses a great exercise with his university students to get
them out of their comfort zone.

    *Every time I object to a stereotype that someone else
applies to me or to someone else, I'm aware of my own
biases. It is my immediate reflex to judge a person
based on their bias. But for every action, there is an
equal and opposite reaction. It is a natural human
reaction to defend your ground, to defend your own
viewpoint. But there's often a fine line between a viewpoint and a bias.*

    *I now teach journalism at Virginia Common-
wealth University. Each year, I give a lecture on the*

controversy over Richmond's Shockoe Bottom and efforts to locate a baseball stadium on top of a historic area that once was the epicenter of the domestic, wholesale slave trade in this country. The area has never been excavated, but because of how it was developed, we know that many of these sites representing the shame of our nation still exist undisturbed since they were buried more than 100 years ago.

I typically spend nearly an hour walking students through the emotional and fraught history of Shockoe, and of Richmond, as it charts the story of the divergent paths toward liberty for black and white America, in a city that can authentically lay claim to being the place where the foundations were laid for the Constitution and the Bill of Rights, but also where the framework making possible the commercial farming of slaves and the philosophical undergirding of the Confederacy were constructed. This entire history can be told between St. John's Church, the Virginia capitol, the Burial Ground for Negroes, and Rocketts Landing— basically the boundaries of Shockoe Valley.

This emotionally exhausting review typically draws out a couple of tears, and never fails to charge up students who beforehand will profess no interest in history, but who afterwards are ready to lay down in front of bulldozers to prevent the evil hands of developers from destroying this national treasure. When I give this lecture, I make a point of drawing it out so I'm left with just about three minutes to outline the rebuttal—the "other side" of the story. And I ask my students after I finish the history review if they think I can sway them to the other side. The answer is always an emotional no.

I then give a three-minute lecture outlining the challenges that have been created by 200 years of development and decay that now prevent revitalizing an area that is the symbolic and physical heart and soul of the city. I explain how and why development in the area is impossible unless flooding can be alleviated—one of the few realistic plans to do so requires building a giant basin, in this case used as a baseball stadium—that will provide a retention pond and drain field for the floodwaters that inevitably destroy the area every 20 to 50 years. And then there are the people who own property, who own businesses, and who try to make the area better today, but who are prevented from realizing their potential.

The students walk out of my class confused, and questioning themselves. Which is the point. They also walk out understanding that context matters, and that there are no bad guys in this modern political drama that pits the preservationists versus the developers. The world certainly has bad guys who come along now and then, but most of the time there are only protagonists—and everyone is fighting for what they think is right.

Activity #4 – Devil's Advocate

Flex your debate muscles and find a friend or family member you trust. The best partner for this game is someone who makes you laugh or has some kind of theatre background. Your job is to choose a topic, preferable not a hot-button topic at first, and argue the side you *don't* agree with for at least five minutes. Invite your partner to argue the side you would typically support. If you took forensics or debate in school, you should be good at this. Talk out your emotional response to the activity. If you can't think of a good person to help with this exercise, then write a letter to yourself advocating for the opposing view. Or video record your perspective and watch it

Activity #4 increases your critical thinking skills. Some of the most successful leaders in the world are able to see all sides of an issue and synthesize perspectives into solutions that work for everyone. Of course there is always some compromise, but when you can really see someone else's perspective and validate their view even a little, it goes a long way toward building bridges across difference.

When you engage in this sort of work, it's important to beware the temptation of remaining in the soft embrace of a comfort zone. You know what we mean: it's when we naturally gravitate only toward people just like ourselves. Why? Because it's *easy*, the path of least resistance! Matthew Freeman has some great examples of noticing how this in-group phenomenon shaped the world in which he grew up.

I was raised in the affluent suburbs of Richmond, Virginia. I wasn't there because my family was rich; I was there because my father was a white United Methodist pastor and the denomination, at that time, assigned pastors primarily to churches where they were racially similar to the congregation. The west end of Richmond, River Road specifically, is very affluent and fairly homogeneous. In fact, it was designed that way on purpose. Most of the neighborhood had been built

45

during the height of white flight. The church I grew up in had, in fact, relocated from the downtown core to the suburbs in the 1960s. Members included a governor, a Fortune 500 CEO, business owners, doctors, and law-yers. I sometimes find it surprising that, having grown up surrounded by such wealth and privilege, I ended up doing the kind of work I do and writing a book like this.

Maybe some of you reading this book are from a similarly homogeneous background, surrounded by those from a similar racial, educational, and socioeconomic background. Making small but deliberate choices to expand your access to different people and ideas is all that's needed to begin the process of notic-ing and moving out of your comfort zone.

A series of small steps each led me further and further away from the kind of environment I was comfortable with and introduced me to new kinds of people. I went to college 45 minutes from where I grew up, at the Col-lege of William and Mary, not a risky choice. But there I sought out people who disagreed with me for conver-sation and friendship. I joined both a hard-partying fraternity and a weekly Christian Bible study. I inten-tionally chose classes that challenged my received notions of how the world worked. And when I decided to go to graduate school, I chose to leave the South in order to gain some critical distance on the culture in which I'd been raised. In my search for grad schools, I came across a seminary that had the programs I was interested in plus an incredible mix of faculty and stu-dents from all over the globe. And so I took the step to attend Regent College, a part of the University of Brit-ish Columbia, in Vancouver, Canada.

At Regent, I learned theology from a Brit, sociology from an Australian, and history from a Canadian who was the descendant of Russian Mennonites who fled to the prairies of Canada to escape religious persecution. As a teaching assistant for that history professor, I typed up his translations of letters from the early 1900s, written by these Russian communities seeking sanctuary around the globe. And I learned, with some surprise, that many of them wanted to avoid coming to the United States because it was not perceived as welcoming and tolerant of newcomers, and they were unsure whether they would have the religious freedom they sought as Christian pacifists who wanted to avoid forced military service. At 22 years old, I had sadly only encountered a narrative that proclaimed the United States as "the greatest nation on earth," and that "everyone wants to come here." Living in Canada, a country that from its early days welcomed dissenters from the American Revolution who wanted to stay loyal to the crown, reshaped my narrow perspective on American exceptionalism.

Learning history from the other side of the border helped Matthew realize how narrow his perspectives were, how much they had been shaped by an in-group dynamic that shared only stories from their own viewpoint. It also opened his eyes to the reality that people from diverse backgrounds could help him uncover assumptions he didn't even know he held.

I also learned from my fellow students. I was in a weekly community group with Nigerians, Germans, Chinese, and New Zealanders. For the first semester we took turns each week sharing our life stories. I learned just how sheltered I had been in the privileged enclaves I'd inhabited in Virginia. While American Christians complain about religious persecution when corporations say "Happy Holidays" instead of "Merry Christmas," my Nigerian friend shared what it was like to live in a country where Christians and Muslims have been killing each other for decades. My friends from Hong Kong talked about their fear for the future economic and religious freedom in their city since China had taken back control from the British. And my Canadian friends and neighbors taught me about how differently other countries approach social challenges from poverty, to drug addiction, to violence, than the Southern American context I was from.

I also learned, in more mundane ways, just how deeply culture shapes each of us. I'll never forget when my German friends, Henning and Cornelia Grossman, asked, "Do you not like us?" I was shocked! We hung out several times a week, shared coffee and dinner regularly. How could they think I didn't like them?

"Of course I do," I replied. "Why would you even ask that question?"

"Because whenever you come over, you're always 10 minutes late."

A light bulb went off. I was taught, through experience if not through words, that it's polite to arrive just a few minutes after the invitation time. That way the host won't be frazzled and has just a minute to catch their breath after finishing the cooking, cleaning, or whatever pre-event details need attending. My German friends, on the other hand, see timeliness as a sign of respect, and would often show up 5 to 10 minutes early, causing me a great deal of panic and last-minute scrambling to get food on the table. In my book, they were not just 10 minutes early, but 20! I wasn't expecting them until 10 minutes late. And in theirs, I was 20 minutes late, as they expected me to be early. And it was these kind of subtle, daily interactions with people who were different from me in some way that revealed to me the depth of assumptions that I presumed were more widely shared than they were.

Even these kinds of simple differences can raise far deeper questions about why we believe the way we do. We are all shaped, more deeply than we can fathom, by the context in which we live. Our families, religious communities, neighborhoods, countries— they all form a context that teaches you how to interpret the actions and behaviors of those around you. Matthew continues:

Is showing up late to a party a sign of disrespect? Or is it polite? Or is it a manipulative way to declare your relative importance vis-à-vis those who have invited you to their gathering? Is it OK to date outside of your race? Your faith? Your nationality? What about adopting children from a race or nation other than your own?

While in graduate school I participated in an informal, coffee-shop debate with a Bolivian and a couple from Poland. The question on the table: Should you return land to people whose ancestors had it stolen from them? The Bolivian passionately argued that yes, Spanish colonialists had stolen land from the indigenous peoples of Bolivia, and the current poverty and destitution afflicting native peoples was a direct result of this history of land theft. Justice required figuring out some way to redistribute the land.

Incidentally, this has been tried with varying levels of success in multiple postcolonial societies, including South Africa. The response from the Polish couple: nonsense. The borders between Germany and Poland have shifted so many times over the past century, not to mention millennia, that it would be an act of foolishness to renegotiate current borders and land claims. History is full of injustice, and we cannot possibly undo all the mistakes of the past. If our sense of justice is predicated on that, we are doomed to failure.

For Matthew, it was fascinating to see how each position was defensible, both morally and logically, but was also completely bound up in the cultural and historical context in which these folks lived. It is only through encounters with others that we can begin to see how and to what extent we ourselves have been shaped by our context.

So how can you discover your assumptions? By expanding your in-group. Meet people different to you and talk to them—about anything really, but don't avoid the hard stuff.

Activity #5 – Get Out of the Zone

It's going to be fine. We know it's intimidating, but you have to get a little uncomfortable to get good at building authentic relationships. Find a place where you will be in the minority, the more extreme the better. Try being the only _____ (fill in the blank) person in a large group of other folks. Journal your thoughts, feelings, and conversations. It can be very eye opening, sometimes for the better and sometimes for the worse. Don't let one experiment shape your perspective forever. Rinse, repeat, and see how the experience of being out of your comfort zone evolves.

In the words of our friend Doug Brown:

As a white male in the US, it is often difficult to cross racial and cultural lines without committing some kind of wrong. Some people of color say Caucasians shouldn't teach children of color, or live in neighborhoods that historically have been for people of color, or parent children of color, or sing music by people of color, and who am I to disagree? Yet, I think we must step into some places where we don't quite belong, with love and with our eyes, ears, and hearts stretched wide open.

Can expanding your in-group really help you overcome bias? The research on unconscious bias is relatively new, and the research on overcoming it newer still. Although more is needed, the path toward de-biasing seems fairly clear: exposing yourself to counter-stereotype examples leads to at least a temporary decrease in implicit bias scores on the IAT. And although it is entirely possible to have people in your life about whom you hold stereotypes—we all know sexist men who love their wives or the prejudiced woman who "has a black friend"—if you follow our prescriptions to *both* expand your circle *and* check your privilege, research is pointing to this two-part move as key to overcoming bias.

CALL TO ACTION

Meet people where they are if you want them to experience your sincerity and you want to experience theirs. Move out of your comfort zone and into theirs.

Chapter Four

Check your privilege

(and your ego)

There would be no bias if there were no differences. You can't overcome bias if you can't acknowledge that other people see the world differently than you do. And in order to do that, you must recognize that your perspective is not the only one, and that you are highly unlikely to be right all the time. That means checking your ego, and also acknowledging your privilege. Unchecked bias can look like privilege, so it's important to take the time to differentiate the two.

It doesn't matter who you are: if you are reading this book, you are privileged in some way. Privilege, in this context, simply means an advantage available to one group that isn't available to everyone. You, for example, can read. According to UNESCO, that alone puts you ahead of 10 to 20 percent of people over age 15 worldwide. Why the 10 percent disparity? If you are a man, you are more likely to be literate.

Generally speaking, privilege blinds you to the challenges that others face. Suffering through a challenge helps you build empathy for others in a similar situation. So, for example, if you or a loved one has suffered through a chronic illness, you're more likely to identify with the pain of another in a similar situation. The privilege of relative health doesn't make you a bad person, but it makes it harder (but not impossible!) to understand the daily complexities and challenges of navigating life with a chronic condition. And so it is with identity-based privilege. If you've never feared being mistreated by the police because of the color of your skin, it can be challenging to fully understand the constant fear that haunts many people of color in their interactions with law enforcement. If we are to build authentic relationships across difference, we must do the hard work of recognizing our privilege so we can navigate the resulting blind spots more thoughtfully. The starting point is, once again, self-awareness.

● **Know your advantages or risk tripping all over them.**

When it comes to overcoming bias, your ego is not your friend. Your ego needs to feel better than others. Tell it to shut up. Practically, this means suspending judgment and expanding curiosity. If a coworker tells you about a situation where she felt she was treated differently as a woman, there are (at least) two possible responses: (1) "I'm sure that wasn't it. Our manager is on the diversity team, he's not sexist!" Or (2) "I'm sorry you experienced that. Tell me more about what happened." In the end, building relationships across differences requires more responses like number two, where you leave aside, at least temporarily, your own interpretations of the world in order to really understand other interpretations.

So obviously, the conversation about privilege is fraught with tension. First of all, don't freak out if you are a white male. People have hijacked the privilege discussion and used it as a weapon to blame and shame white people, especially white men. If you are feeling a sense of guilt, shame, and fear about bias conversations, especially about race, it is not necessary. We are sorry that the United States in particular has made it scary and dangerous for people to express, own, or explore their bias and the world's bias. That is a shame. But just as we have told countless white people we have worked with, *by the power vested in us (by virtue of Tiffany's negritude and our combined dedication to racial reconciliation), we hereby absolve you of your white guilt.* Now don't get all excited and start throwing around slurs and crazy talk. We are just saying that we are fully aware that you did not personally create racism. As far as we know, no one alive on the planet today did. So if that's your deal, let it go.

● **White guilt is paralyzing. If you have it, let it go. You are absolved!**

Here is the catch: You are still responsible for owning your part in society's contemporary issues. You are not completely off the hook. But then again, neither are we.

Tiffany explains privilege from her perspective.

Even as a black woman, I have a great deal of privilege. Privilege is not and never has been the exclusive territory of one race, gender, or other group of people. Privilege is relative. Now please don't hear what I am not saying. I am not saying that white, male, Christian, US citizens, like my coauthor Matthew, are not privileged. I am just stating that they are not alone in their privilege and therefore should not be made to feel an exclusive sense of guilt for what their ancestors did 400 years ago. Yes, it was horrible. Yes, the legacy of slavery and misogyny persists today. So rather than blame the folks who didn't start the mess, why don't we all work together toward clear, mutually beneficial solutions? I say mutually beneficial solutions because addressing bias on an interpersonal level, when done on a large scale, can actually begin to affect larger systems. When people get all bent out of shape about privilege and who does and does not have it, it's usually the larger systems that are the source of the frustration.

● **Privilege is relative. Anyone can have it, and most everyone has some.**

Intuitively, most people understand that our societal biases did not begin last week. People are upset because women are still paid less than men in the United States on average *even though we all know that it's wrong and unfair*. So why is this obviously unfounded bias still allowed to affect real people in really unfortunate ways? Because the systems that support it were built on bias, and that has been very deeply embedded into everything. Unraveling racism, sexism, xenophobia, ableism, and other pernicious biases will require the collective effort of very thoughtful and deliberate people. So if you aspire to be among those change makers and want to help your friends, associates, and family members join our ranks, get ready to own your privilege and use it for good.

Activity #6 – The Power of Privilege TEDx Talk
This one is easy. Just type "Tiffany Jana TED Talk" into a search engine and watch Tiffany's TEDx Talk. Why read what I have to say about it when you can watch it online!

● **Identify your privilege and use it for good wherever you see bias.**

The good news is that mutually beneficial solutions are possible because everyone ultimately wins when inclusion is realized. We like to think that our work of bringing people together across differences will be done when race is no longer predictive of outcome, when the fallacy of the hierarchy of human value is as well understood as the fact that the earth is round. We look forward to the day when kids will read about how we used to think some people were inherently better than others and they will think, "That's so silly!"

The other challenge with the privilege conversation is that the mention of it puts people on the defensive. You definitely want to avoid pain and oppression Olympics. Pain Olympics refers to the human tendency to deny privilege and focus on all the ways you and/or your people's pain is worse than someone else's. That is a no-win proposition. Instead, try applying the control/conquer/prevail framework to your perspective on your own privilege.

1. Neutralize your privilege by acknowledging it. You need not be ashamed nor apologize for the advantages you have, whether they are earned, unearned, inherited, blessed, or otherwise. They are yours and have helped you arrive where you are. Own it. No one can use it against you if you are aware of it, own it, and, perhaps, use it to further more than just your own agenda. (More on that later in the next activity.)

2. Conquer the power privilege has over you by shifting the accusatory/defensive tone to one of questioning, understanding, and empathy. People who point fingers and accuse are often in pain and want to be heard. So try listening. Put your perspective and privilege aside and spend as much time as possible listening and learning without being defensive. Take in someone else's pain and perspective. We promise you, it will not negate your pain, your privilege, your identity, or your experience. It will bring you closer to people, and isn't human connection something we are ultimately seeking?

3. Now this is the hard part—prevailing. Prevailing over privilege requires that we move ourselves aside and listen,

learn, and work in service of others. We don't mean to go all Mother Teresa on you, but that is indeed what a person who moves all of their privilege aside and uses it in favor of others looks like. The masters of prevailing over privilege are self-sacrificial and they are the people who instigate world-changing movements. They are the Gandhis, Martin Luther Kings, and every saint ever. So that's a ridiculously high bar, but the point is, this is a scalable concept. Interpersonally, if you apply these ideas, you will wind up with a fabulously diverse network of friends and associates. At its highest level, you will instigate a change in the way your company, industry, or nation handles bias. That is no small proposition. Don't believe us? Here's a more realistic case study for anyone who isn't ready for sainthood just yet. . . .

Once upon a time, Bart Houlahan led an athletics apparel company with a social mission. The company was AND1, and when you bought a pair of athletic shoes, the company donated a pair to a child who needed a pair of shoes. Sound familiar? Yeah, Bart did that way before TOMS became known for that business model. Bart is a white man, and most of the kids who benefitted from his company's social mission came from low-income families. Bart saw a need within a group that he considered an in-group, so he used his privilege to affect a positive change. Bart worked tirelessly to build a better kind of business, and although it was a for-profit, it was also socially responsible and making a difference in too many ways to name here.

Before long, AND1 had celebrity endorsements and was purchased by a top athletic apparel brand. One of the first things the new owner did was abandon the social mission and stop giving away product. After all, free shoes don't maximize shareholder value. Needless to say, Bart was devastated. He was essentially punished for being successful, so he set out to do something radically different. Bart teamed up with Jay Coen Gilbert and Andrew Kassoy to start a nonprofit called B Lab. B Lab allows social enterprises to take advantage of a new legal form, the benefit corporation, and makes it possible for them to balance shareholder value with social benefit. It supports those businesses and promotes their success through B Corp certification and enhancing their access to capital. By the time this book is published, there will be almost 2,000 certified B Corps worldwide. One man's experience and three friendships forged between Stanford University roommates ignited a global movement that is quantifiably making the world a better place.

● **Privilege does not make anyone better than anyone else. We truly are equals.**

So how do we get there? How do we build so many bridges between people that we finally become one human race? Building authentic relationships requires the individual to purposefully seek out diverse relationships. Being open to relationships is an act of vulnerability and not a welcome setting for egos. Overcoming bias requires becoming a cultural ally—someone who deliberately deepens her or his understanding of others through cultural fluency and cultural competence. Casual, superficial acquaintances are no longer enough.

Consider the most inclusive people you know; the ones whose social circles look like the United Nations. Those people have often allowed themselves the privilege of authentic connection across differences. Sometimes it's a life-altering experience, like participation in the Peace Corps. Connections are often forged when our own privilege is put in perspective if we can put ego aside.

Our friend Myra Goodman Smith has one of the most diverse networks of friends and associates that we have ever seen. Her relationships do not feel false or forced. She has a calm, casual demeanor and she interacts with equal enthusiasm with all the people we have seen who trust and respect her as a leader and a friend. Here is what she has to say about her experiences building authentic relationships across difference.

I can truly say that I have more diverse relationships than anyone I know. I am president and CEO of Leadership Metro Richmond, our region's community leadership development and engagement organization. LMR began in 1980 as an innovative program to improve racial, gender, and socioeconomic divides in our area's community leadership.

In response, a group of visionary leaders were recruited to participate in a new program designed to connect diverse groups of emerging leaders for greater understanding and cooperation. The group employed thoughtful examination of the challenges within the community and gathered multiple perspectives on these challenges while creating a safe environment of understanding and respect for the viewpoints of others. Those 42 community leaders became the first Leadership Metro Richmond class. Thirty-five years later, LMR has evolved into a galvanized network of over 1,900 diverse leaders/members, with 1,400 still residing in our region.

My role is to serve and lead LMR members who represent various demographic cohorts: race, ethnicity, gender, age, wealth, religion, political party, educational levels, and residence. Many of our members come to me for coaching, advising, and guidance on issues of community leadership, personal growth, and just tackling the day-to-day issues of life. They all have their own uniqueness and differences, yet their desires and concerns are very similar. I show them respect (my core value) and recognize their uniqueness.

When asked what significant moments in her life journey brought Myra to her current position, she responded:

I love leadership. As a child, I read every biography on the bookmobile . . . books on leaders and history makers from all backgrounds. I learned about their struggles and accomplishments, which provided clarity in why they acted, interacted, and made decisions the way they did. Understanding more about people than what I see has been a lifelong driver for me.

I truly believe in relationships across differences, which was not and still is not embraced by all. A year after the integration of schools, one of my new best friends was white. The youthful verbal hate I received only made me more resolved to have relationships with individuals different than me. Today, I tell folks that I have the most diverse network of friends ever. . . . I say it with a huge smile. I have learned so much from them and realize even more that they see me and not the difference.

Some people become cultural allies after prolonged exposure to someone they care about who is a member of a marginalized demographic—a homosexual sister, a close friend who relies on a wheelchair. Experiencing profoundly personal situations, whether directly or indirectly, has a way of opening minds and hearts. Again, when we have close relationships with people who experience privilege differently, our perspective changes. We propose that you don't wait for diversity to smack you in the face. It's everywhere. Seek it out, check your ego, get out of your comfort zone, and get to know people who are different from you.

As a white, male, heterosexual, business-owning American citizen, Matthew has enjoyed societal advantages based on his identities. It can be challenging for people with privilege like Matthew to see it and acknowledge it. Conversations about privilege often make those who have some feel morally responsible for the inequalities in the world, or seem to call into question their accomplishments in life, attributing them to unchosen identities instead of hard work. Learning to see the privilege you have is an essential step in building relationships across difference, particularly where one person belongs to a socially marginalized group. Here's how Matthew thinks about his own privilege:

I have a lot of privilege. How did I get it? It wasn't from some pre-birth privilege shopping spree where I chose the identities I wanted off a celestial shelf. Privilege, or the lack of it, is about what is done to you by society— it's about which societal in-groups are valued and appreciated, and whose experiences are considered mainstream and normal.

I once guest-lectured in a high school friend's college classroom. Bryan was, at the time, a professor in a small liberal arts school in Pennsylvania and asked me to come and talk about, among other things, privilege. So I asked the students to brainstorm a list of groups that are, in some way, marginalized in American society. Here's what they generated:

Marginalized Groups
1. People of color
2. Women
3. People with disabilities
4. People in poverty
5. LGBT people
6. Non-Christians
7. Immigrants

I then asked the students to think about, if these folks were on the margins of society, who were the corresponding groups that we might think of as being in the "center." Their list:

Marginalized Groups	Center
1. People of color	1. White people
2. Women	2. Men
3. People with disabilities	3. Able-bodied people
4. People in poverty	4. People not in poverty
5. LGBT people	5. Heterosexuals
6. Non-Christians	6. Christians
7. Immigrants	7. Natural-born US citizens

I then asked a question that took some courage on my part given how emotionally and politically fraught conversations about privilege are, even though its answer is fairly obvious. I asked the students to think about me, their guest lecturer, and point out which categories I fell into in the marginalized groups vs. the center. Visually obvious to them was that I was a white, able-bodied man who did not appear to be in poverty by virtue of my clothing and appearance as a guest lecturer visiting from another state. Obvious from my stories was that I was born in the United States, into a Christian family, and that I was married to a woman. There was not a single one of these examples in which I fell into a category that is marginalized in twenty-first-century America. I asked the students if my privilege was my choice. Looking at these categories, their answers were "of course not."

From this list, there are arguably only two categories that might be considered some kind of choice. One is religion, the other, wealth. It is worth pointing out, however, that both religion and socioeconomic status are not a choice when you are a child. These early influences are dictated by the choices and circumstances of whoever raised you. Nevertheless, I used this exercise as a launchpad to talk about my experiments in choosing voluntary poverty, in part as an attempt to make the choice *to give up some privilege and live in solidarity with people who are often marginalized and ignored.*

But can you actually give up privilege? Well, you can't change your skin color, but you can change your socioeconomic status and choose poverty. Dorothy Day, the founder of the Catholic Worker Movement, once said, "I condemn poverty and I advocate it; poverty is simple and complex at once; it is a social phenomenon and a personal matter."[1] Voluntary poverty is very different from involuntary poverty, and the two should not be confused. For centuries, Buddhist monks, Catholic nuns, and utopian communalists have embraced voluntary poverty as a way to free themselves from the demands of material society to pursue enlightenment. Dorothy Day and the Catholic Workers inspired by her embrace voluntary poverty for an additional reason: as a means to bridge the divide in experience between those who are poor and those who are not. Day said voluntary poverty "means nonparticipation in those comforts and luxuries which have been manufactured by the exploitation of others . . . while our brothers [and sisters] suffer from lack of necessities, we will refuse to enjoy comforts."[2] Matthew was so intrigued by this notion, and inspired by Day's example, he decided to try living in voluntary poverty.

It was, in some ways, another in my series of small steps. I was working at a nonprofit and already not making much money. I was living in a racially mixed lower-middle-class neighborhood, and all I was doing was moving across town to a neighborhood that was more homogeneous—black and mostly poor—and committing to maintaining my low income.

I created my own Catholic Worker community house a few blocks from the Fairfield Court public housing community in Richmond, Virginia. The three founders, myself included, worked part-time jobs, enough to pay for housing and utilities, but not much else. We sought to be good friends and neighbors, we hosted three meals a week open to anyone in the neighborhood—not as a feeding program but rather as a community gathering space—and we kept a bedroom open for hospitality for anyone in short-term need.

In this house, I learned what it was like to live in an old (nineteenth century) home that had not been maintained, had poor electrical wiring, no working fireplaces, and no insulation. Inside, it was over 100 degrees in the summer, and drafty and cold in the winter. Pipes froze and sometimes burst. I spent many mornings clearing out dead animals from the crawl space so I could use a hairdryer to thaw pipes under the one working bathroom. We couldn't afford contractors, so we bartered with friends who had more skills than we did, tried to learn how to make repairs ourselves, and learned to swallow our pride and accept help from friends and neighbors. I started to see how much I had taken for granted before—running water, comfortable interior temperatures, a house that was a safe space and not full of potential hazards. Neighbors told stories about people they knew who figured out how to steal water or electricity when they couldn't afford the bills.

Taking a step to intentionally set aside some of your privilege can yield a wealth of unexpected insights. We all know the experience of being grateful for electricity after a prolonged power outage. Similarly, choosing to place yourself physically in a space where everyone does not have the same background as you creates shared experiences that lead to an easier path to building authentic relationships.

Depending on how far outside of your comfort zone you step, the experiences can become quite harrowing. Stories from international aid workers and journalists regularly drive this point home, with the reality of kidnappings or violence as an unfortunately common threat. You don't have to leave the United States, however, to experience dangerous situations. Matthew continues:

One night, the police stopped me while I was walking down my street. I looked out of place as a white person in a black neighborhood. Most white people who ventured into this neighborhood were there to buy drugs or sex, and I found myself fitting a criminal profile for the first time in my life. I wish I could say I used the interaction to engage the officer in a conversation on bias, assumptions, profiling, and the difficulties of police work, but instead I succumbed to my fear of an authority figure with power to arrest me, or worse, and showed my ID and only answered questions I was asked.

Despite constant police presence, gunshots rang out nightly. One evening I pulled into the gas station a few blocks from home and noticed a young white man with South Carolina license plates and his car hood propped open. I decided to caution him about the neighborhood, that he was clearly not from here and should therefore keep his wits about him. He said, "Oh I figured that out from the drive-by shooting that just happened." I turned to look where he was pointing, at the gas pumps 100 feet away, just as four cop cars came pulling in lights and sirens blazing.

Another time, the unusual midday gunshots I heard from my bedroom were from a running gun battle that killed an innocent bystander, an elementary school child on his way home from school. My 16-year-old next-door neighbor was a great student who eventually went to college, but in high school he couldn't walk the five blocks to his local school because fights and violence were too likely.

It was, geographically, a short 10 miles from the house I grew up in. But experientially, it's hard to imagine a much different environment. To most of us, these stories sound sadly familiar from the news. But I can tell you, it's one thing to know in your mind that

American cities are plagued by gun violence, but it's a far different thing to have to drop and hit the ground on your own front porch when you hear nearby gunfire, or to receive a phone call that your mentee from the local high school was killed before he could graduate. Living in the midst of poverty and violence damages your soul, and as recent neurological research shows, it damages the brains of children as well.[3]

Nevertheless, while living in this neighborhood, I forged closer and more meaningful relationships than I had for the other 10 years I'd lived in Richmond as an adult. I was invited to Super Bowl parties, Thanksgiving dinners, backyard cookouts. My friend Nate taught me to patch and hang drywall. I learned to garden from a neighbor creating a community garden down the block. We helped our neighbors and were helped by them.

One concrete lesson I learned was that not having money to buy solutions to all of life's problems makes you rely on other people—for better and for worse. I also learned how expensive it is to be poor—to be unable to afford routine maintenance on houses or cars and still have to fix the ensuing expensive disasters somehow. Or the friend who couldn't afford to pay the fines necessary to get his driver's license back, and therefore couldn't find steady work in a city that lacks decent public transit, therefore rendering him unable to pay off the fines, trapping him in a vicious cycle.

So back to our earlier invitations: take yourself out of your comfort zone; make yourself the minority. My stint living in a community house in an impoverished Richmond neighborhood was a radical version of that, one I do not recommend to everyone. For me, however, it was the culmination of a series of much smaller steps to engage with people whose lives were different from my own. And it would fill several books to chronicle what I learned from the experience, and how much my own biased assumptions about people in poverty were obliterated by living alongside them.

Your small steps don't need to be so extreme, but if you really want to see how privilege blinds you to the reality of others, you have to take at least one step to, momentarily, set it aside, make yourself uncomfortable, and go someplace where your experience is not the norm.

As a final note, and an attempt to answer the earlier question about whether you can truly give up your privilege, the answer is of course complicated. Did Matthew have less privilege living in substandard housing amidst gun violence than when living in affluent suburbia? Absolutely. Did he have the connections and privilege to be able to make more money and leave the neighborhood at will? Yes, and when personal tragedy visited his life he did just that. No one can erase his or her privilege entirely and honestly, and you shouldn't try.

What you can do, and what we all must do, regardless of how much privilege we have, is seek to expand our empathy and understanding of people whose lives are different from our own. And we absolutely must use whatever privilege we have to try to create a world where students can no longer easily generate a long list of marginalized people.

CALL TO ACTION

Don't try to deny or ignore your privilege. Just use it for others.

Chapter Five

Scan to expand means keeping your eyes open and looking for opportunities to broaden your cultural horizons. This is where building authentic relationships across differences comes into play. Chapter 3 was about in-groups and out-groups. Those often exist intact without any effort. Scanning to expand is about making a deliberate effort to notice individual differences and really pushing the limits of building bridges across them. This is not the time to be colorblind, gender neutral, or to experience the world as a melting pot with everything ending up a gooey, formless, grey blob.

When you enter an event, do you immediately look around for the people you already know and make a beeline for them? Most of us do. There is comfort in the familiar. What we are suggesting is that you deliberately and actively seek out opportunities that will expose you to new people, new ideas, and new places.

Remember contact theory? We designed "scan to expand" in response to the research that tells us we can reduce interpersonal bias by spending protracted amounts of time with people about whom we have known or unknown bias. If you chose to take the Implicit Association Test and identified one or more potential biases, then you should consider scanning your environment for opportunities to work or play in group settings with people who represent the categories you identified as a demographic where you could reduce your bias.

For instance, the organization Myra Smith is in charge of, Leadership Metro Richmond, offers exactly the type of opportunity for bias reduction that contact theory suggests. LMR participants work with each other for nine months, learning about leadership and their community and ultimately working in smaller teams on a sustainable community project. Though everyone who participates is some kind of leader, there are no hierarchies in the program. We helped fund a scholarship for a young man in his twenties to participate in 2015. He learned and worked alongside executive directors and CEOs. What matters most is the differences are used to improve the leaders' service to the community. A wide variety of races, colors, religions, ages, genders, sexual orientations, and socioeconomic statuses is part of any given LMR class. It's the diversity and the shared goals that enrich the experience for everyone.

● *Having authentic relationships with people who think differently is the key to overcoming your bias.*

Privilege can blind you to the experiences of others, or cause you to misunderstand their experiences, choices, and opinions. The good news is that we can break down those walls through intentionally cultivating diverse friendships and experiences for ourselves. You just have to be intentional about it. The world is a naturally diverse place. Even if you live in a seemingly homogeneous community, diversity itself is bigger than the constrained definitions we often use. Yes, having friends and an in-group comprised of people who *look* different is a great first step. But differences are something you want in your in-groups in whatever form they take.

● *Don't be afraid to expose your family and friends to new people and ideas.*

The in-group concept works at any level of relationships. The nuclear family can be an in-group in relation to a neighborhood—think "stranger danger." Street gangs, often formed by the block, can be the in-group relative to the gang on the next block. Cultural, racial, political, or national identity can all constitute in-groups or out-groups depending on whose perspective you consider. In-groups give us a sense of belonging, of identity, but as history has shown us again and again, they can also lead to exclusion and violence.

It can often be challenging to shake up the in-group in a family setting. How often do we stop and fret about the guest list at a family gathering or wonder whether one or more relatives will make a certain guest feel uncomfortable? Disrupting the status quo is hard. Unfortunately, it is simply not enough for us to be inclusive ourselves. We cannot sit around and lament the state of the world and expect someone else to fix it. Don't be ashamed of your diverse relationships. Give your family and friends a chance to see what you see in people who are different from them. If each of us helps one other person expand their cultural horizons and rethink their bias, the impact on society would be tremendous.

● **Know your in-groups, then start including out-group members to reduce interpersonal bias.**

Workplaces are fantastic learning labs for inclusive behavior. The good news is that there is no need to overthink it. The scan to expand solution will take you out of your comfort zone, but that is only temporary. Human beings are resilient. Once you adjust to the new status quo, it won't be so uncomfortable anymore.

Anyone who has management or supervisory status has the opportunity to scan to expand. There are countless ways that a supervisor can create an inclusive workplace. Here are a few:

1. Create diverse teams by assigning people to them with diverse skills, strengths, and backgrounds. This means you must familiarize yourself with people's strengths.

2. Seek input from everyone you supervise regardless of organizational level or title.

3. Find ways to implement all or part of concepts that your teams generate.

4. Recognize employees for their unique contributions.

If you are an individual contributor at your workplace, you can also make inclusive decisions that help you expand your network and cultural understanding and reduce any interpersonal bias you may have identified. Here are some possibilities:

1. Volunteer to join diverse teams and committees.

2. Out yourself as a cultural ally by standing up when biased comments are made.

3. Seek out the opinions of your colleagues from your out-group.

4. Make suggestions that are respectful of the opinions, experiences, and perspectives of your out-groups.

5. Expand the list of people you invite to work-related or after-work outings.

These activities will help you build workplace relationships that can help expand your cultural horizons. High emotional intelligence and cultural competency are leadership skills that can help you get recognized and promoted in the workplace. Inclusion really is a win-win practice.

● **You don't have to be born into diversity and inclusion; you can choose it.**

The key is to keep your eyes open and look for opportunities to expand your horizons. Once you start looking, you will see ways to expand your in-group everywhere you go.

The authors of this book experienced in-group expansion firsthand starting from an early age. Tiffany, for instance, grew up multilingual.

My friends and babysitters spoke Spanish, so I picked up the language before I learned English. I always felt a sense of home and belonging with Mexican people because I had close, personal relationships with them for as long as I could remember. As an army brat, I traveled the world with my parents and learned that people are both similar and different everywhere you go. I attended German elementary school, learned a third language, and expanded my "family" to include a whole European nation. My friends were Turkish, German, Czech, French, Spanish, Vietnamese, Muslim, Catholic, and more. Befriending a diverse group of people changed the way I experience individuals and the world. Feeling like a member of a much broader community than my African American peers ultimately led me to diversity work.

My early experiences led me to seek out diverse friendships and uncomfortable situations. I learned to love being the only black person in a room, or the only English speaker. It was disconcerting in the beginning, but then it became an adventure. Gaining friends, hearing their stories, and becoming part of their adventures have created a mind-expanding, joy-filled journey.

Matthew's in-group expansion was a more deliberate decision he made in his adult life.

I expanded my in-group through an employment opportunity. When I moved back home to Richmond,

Virginia, after five years in Vancouver, I was looking for meaningful work opportunities that would allow me to use my skills and tap into my passion for social justice. In the process, I met Rev. Brian Brown, an African-American United Methodist pastor who was leading his church in a racial reconciliation ministry. He offered me the chance to be his assistant, working in a black church for racial reconciliation.

I respectfully declined. Although I passionately believed we needed to make progress on race relations, I had sworn I was not going to work in a church. I was a pastor's kid. I had no illusions about what church work was like—lots of late-night committee meetings and hours of thankless toiling behind the scenes while many folks think you only work an hour on Sunday morning. No thank you. I wanted to have a bigger impact than working in a single church. Besides, I had questions about my own faith, so I wasn't sure I should be a church leader if I didn't have it all figured out.

Reverend Brown heard my objections, and he overruled them. In the most helpful way, he encouraged me to think about this as a part of a journey, not necessarily the destination. And most importantly, he encouraged me to see this as an invaluable opportunity to expand my in-group.

And so it was that I worked in an African American church, leading worship, sometimes preaching, occasionally playing the piano as, usually, the only white person in the room. It was a transformative experience. I cannot tell you how many times I felt uncomfortable, out of my element, lost for words, unsure of whether my experience was relevant and worth sharing. But I always felt accepted, loved, and welcomed. And though I'm no longer at that church, I still count many of its members as friends today. Whether it's through in-person conversations, or Facebook posts, or just having attended the same church for four years, the richness of my interpersonal interactions has increased exponentially by taking the opportunity to expand my in-group, even when it was uncomfortable for me.

Our friend Doug Brown took a similar leap of faith and expanded his in-group in a unique and profound way.

The primary way I'm in contact with people different from me has been through my relationship with my children; I adopted my three girls from Perú in 2009. We are a family at this point, well attached and speaking English with little flecks of Spanish thrown in from time to time. We attended the Smithsonian Peruvian festival this past summer. During the day we wandered from booth to booth, taking in bits of culture and eating Peruvian food. I was glad that we stayed for an evening concert, because it was then that the daytime crowd of curious non-Peruvians made way for an evening crowd of almost exclusively Peruvian Americans.

There we were, surrounded by people of Peruvian descent, awash in Eva Ayllón's Peruvian cross-rhythms, and my blue eyes must have been the only pair in the crowd. What I felt at the time was not my own sense of being out of place, but my children's sense of relief in finding something of their birth country and their people—not just a Spanish class in school that mainly caters to Mexican Spanish, or a restaurant that serves one or two Peruvian dishes along with Tex-Mex food, or a dance class that teaches a Cuban dance that has made its way to Perú. I find that parenting children from a lightly represented culture in the US means we connect with their culture in lots of one-off, close-enough ways. On that evening we hit a kind of cultural bull's-eye, and it felt really great.

The decision to adopt internationally was a complicated one, and I'm not sure exactly how I got there. There was a very practical part of me that couldn't reconcile the presence of orphans in the world and a decision to give birth, and the race of a child or children is just one of the many decisions a potential adoptive parent must make. In many ways, one of the first forks in the adoption road is about race: "Do I want to adopt a Caucasian child or a non-Caucasian child?" Neither I, nor my girls' mother, felt strongly about having children of our same race, so we didn't feel the need to pursue Caucasian children. Perú's program looked good to us; the pace was deliberate and logical, and their orphanages had a good reputation for care. We decided that a sibling group would be a sensible way of keeping cultural connections strong in a new country. Looking back, the injustice of international adoption was not as apparent to me then as it is now. It is a sort of emigration without consent, and understanding it as such helps to keep me focused on helping my girls to maintain contact and connection with their home culture.

Doug's decision to scan for ongoing opportunities to keep his daughters exposed to their ethnic culture is a way of keeping the birthright of their ancestral in-group accessible to them. In the process, he has expanded his own in-group and reduced biases he didn't realize he had.

In Perú, all of the necessary squeamishness about water, food, and gastrointestinal survival feels a little funny when your children don't have to worry about those things at all. In the five weeks I spent with them in Perú at the time of their adoption, I realized that many of the things that seemed foreign to me about Peruvian culture were things that felt familiar to my children and how important it would be to remember that feeling of otherness when the children arrived in the US.

Another friend, Heather Crislip, chose a different way to expand her horizons rather than stay in her comfort zone. Heather made a life-changing career choice based on the idea of expanding her impact in the world and her understanding of cultural issues.

After college I had a choice to work in a bank or in New Haven's Welfare Department. I chose to leave my comfort zone and enter a career of public service. I was tremendously attracted to the Welfare Department and the ability to make change for the city's most disadvantaged. New Haven was home to some of the nation's most venerable institutions, but I had never seen chronic poverty and racial segregation like I saw in the Hill neighborhood I worked in, which was nearly entirely African American and had poverty rates that topped 50 percent.

We often talked about A Tale of Two Cities *to describe our work and to empower our clients in the shadow of the nation's elite, which was both poignant and deeply disappointing. I loved the city and realized that just disagreeing or disapproving of the situation would not be enough to make the racism change. The perspective I gained working with those with no options and seeing my community through their eyes has always stayed with me.*

My understanding of poor neighborhoods and the resulting limited choices of those residents was one of the reasons I had the great fortune to move up to serve the mayor of the majority-minority city. Our team was committed to social justice and creating opportunity for marginalized communities, with fair housing and fair rent often utilized as important tools. The year before I left New Haven I worked with the city to update its Fair Housing Analysis of Impediments, which took several months of work. We recommended improved education, outreach, and enforcement of fair housing laws; improved coordination and enforcement between the various departments and agencies involved with housing issues and fair housing choice, including both landlords and tenants; and expanding the availability of housing of all types to make housing available for persons regardless of need.

Doing that work helped me really focus on fair housing and housing choice as a key issue and solution to the cycle of poverty. The lesson I took away from my six years in New Haven was that communities are not what they appear from the outside, and that the cycle of poverty is firmly centered on housing and where you live. It impacts every other aspect of one's life, framing your expectations and your opportunities.

Marianne Vermeer is an entrepreneurial executive who works internationally. Her work and her life involve interacting with people from around the world. She seeks out opportunities where she can do that—she scans to expand. Her family has made their home a place where people from literally anywhere can feel welcome. They have entertained and hosted people of many nationalities, religious persuasions, and political positions. They have "adopted" young adults coming to the US to study or do research and provided them with an American family. And they have legally adopted a son from China so their family life has involved bringing a culture different from the one they were raised in into their family traditions.

Marianne describes herself as follows:

I grew up in a very unidimensional family: we were Dutch. ALL Dutch. Spoke the language, ate the food, prided ourselves on being Dutch. In my young years, we lived in communities with lots of Dutch people. We moved to western Nebraska when I was in kindergarten and all of a sudden we were a bit different—there weren't many Dutch people around. And though I thought I spoke perfect English, I quickly learned that my vocabulary was peppered with Dutch words and people didn't understand me. This was my first experience of feeling different.

And I adapted. I quickly learned which words were only to be used at home and what the English word really was that I should use in other places. Still, it was a small town and I knew there was a bigger world to be found. I couldn't wait to get out of there. For the most part, my childhood world was populated by white people, with a few Hispanics who lived on the other side of the railroad tracks. I applied for the Peace Corps when I was 16 and was told I really needed to finish high school first. My parents convinced me I was more valuable to the world with a college degree so I spent two summers in college working in cross-cultural environments to test my wings: a summer in southeastern Alaska in Native Alaskan villages and logging camps and a second summer in Appalachian southeastern Kentucky.

I did these summer experiences to make sure I could adapt and thrive in environments where I was the one who was different. I ignored my college graduation ceremony in favor of leaving immediately for Egypt for two years to teach English in an Egyptian girls' school. Learned Arabic. Traveled all over Egypt. Took every chance I could to explore the lives of ordinary Egyptians. Spent a summer in a village in southern Egypt where no one spoke English (and I mean NO ONE). Joined friends teaching English to monks in a Coptic Orthodox monastery in the desert on their weekend jaunts out there. Taught English teachers for a month in the Sinai Peninsula on the border with Israel, where the tensions of the Middle East were readily apparent. And I LOVED it. Wasn't sure I wanted to come back to the US, but family concerns brought me back. I retain a fondness for all things Egyptian. I learned I could work well in cross-cultural environments, make friends, learn a language, and retain my identity as an American of Dutch heritage.

How often do you stop and take stock of how diverse and inclusive your life is? Is cultural expansion part of the conversations you typically have with friends, family, and colleagues? Even if it is, try the next activity. It tends to be an eye-opener.

Activity #7 – Diversity Inventory

For your top five friends (folks you trust the most), list each person's race, gender, religion, sexual orientation, socioeconomic status, occupation, and personality type (extrovert, introvert, etc.).

How are they similar to you?

How are they different from you?

What else did you notice?

Some people find that activity challenging, while others think it's easy. There is no correct set of responses. It is simply a tool you can use to raise your awareness about who we choose to have in our lives. There is no need to have a friend quota, but if you never stop to think about the composition of your networks, you will find yourself in the same circles you are in now. That may not be a bad thing at all, but if you want a more diverse network, the first thing you need to do is know your starting point.

● *Your in-group is about more than just people.*

Maybe you don't have opportunities to befriend new people. That's cool. You're still able to scan to expand in order to overcome bias. What you need is a cultural activity inventory:

Activity #8 – Cultural Inventory

List the last three books you read.

List the last three movies you saw.

List a few TV shows you watch.

List your favorite music artists.

For each of these categories, list as best you can the race, gender, religion, and sexual orientation of the musicians, authors, and/or main characters.

How are they similar to you?

How are they different from you?

What else did you notice?

Chimamanda Adichie, a Nigerian author, has a wonderful TED Talk called "The Danger of a Single Story." We highly recommend it and sometimes screen it in our trainings. She talks about how the stories we hear, and those we don't, profoundly shape the way in which we understand other people. As an African she relays her firsthand experience of people's assumptions that she must be poor, and certainly different, and their surprise at her love of Mariah Carey. That surprise stems from the single story we have of the diverse continent of Africa—as she says, we hear only stories of beautiful landscapes and war-torn, impoverished, incomprehensible people. But we don't hear stories of small business entrepreneurs, or authors, or dedicated social justice activists. Which leads us to think of Africans through a simplistic lens. She encourages us to expand the stories we encounter through scanning to expand your reading list, paying attention to who stars in the movies you watch, and who writes them. It is possible to expand your in-group without meeting a single new person.

If you want to make the jump from simply controlling your bias to conquering and eventually prevailing over it, it takes a lifetime of deliberate effort. Remember the appendix syndrome? You can't simply read one Toni Morrison novel, check that off your list, and move on. Just like with hygiene, you must make ongoing, intentional choices to expand your in-group.

Marianne Vermeer shares the following insight on how intentional choices helped build relationships across differences.

When we went to Pakistan, we consciously told ourselves we were going to love the people of that country. And we set out to do just that. For the first year, we invited someone for dinner in our home every Friday evening and asked them to tell us about their families, their religion, their thoughts on the future of their country. It was a safe place to come—we promised that nothing would leave our living room and that we wanted to learn as much as we could. When someone invited us to his/her home, we made every effort to accept the invitation. We loved those folks—and still do. So my advice is to decide you want to build those relationships and make them work. Be authentic about it.

Regardless of education or language, people can read when someone is not sincere. Realize that your attempts may require more of you than of others in the relationship but that the friendship will become more of a two-way street when the others realize you are sincere and interested in their lives. That can take a while. Read newspapers or blogs from the other person's culture, country, or community. Find books or websites that talk about the history of their community, culture, country, religion—whatever defines them. Be vulnerable. Realize it doesn't always work—is there ever a perfect relationship among human beings? People don't always "click"—that's OK. Keep trying. . . . I promise you there are many people wanting to have engaged friendships and supportive relationships in the world. And your life will be richer for having them as friends.

A special note to parents: Your children will only be able to be culturally competent and unbiased if you have these conversations with them and teach them inclusive skills. Bias is the default human condition. We cannot tell you how often concerned parents reach out to us and ask how their children could have become so culturally insensitive when they are great parents who fight for social justice. It happens because their families don't discuss things like racism, sexism, homophobia, and other biases. The fact that you traveled internationally and don't have a xenophobic bone in your body does not mean that your children will inherit that from you. Marianne Vermeer made sure her kids understood the gravity of her international and inclusive perspective by taking her children overseas.

After 20 years of largely living and working in the US, I wanted to go back overseas at a time when my children could experience another culture, learn the language, and challenge their assumptions about how the world works. After some fits and starts, our family sold nearly everything we owned in 2005 and, with two suitcases each and a trombone, moved to Lahore, Pakistan, for three years. Our purpose was to help rebuild a Christian college there after 30 years of government control. The culture shock was deep and real, the challenges daunting. And we thrived! We consider Pakistan our second home and find ways to remain in touch with the many friends we made there. My work since that time has focused on bringing my business skills to organizations that want to grow and create impact. This has taken me back to South Asia, to East Africa, and to organizations around the US. I've been a staff member, a consultant, a CEO, and an entrepreneur.

Of course everyone can't take their kids overseas to live, but we can make choices that help them see the world more comprehensively. Discuss what's happening on the world stage. Ask your kids their opinions about challenging topics early while their minds are still flexible. If you don't do the hard, often uncomfortable, work of molding your kids' perspectives, the rest of the world will do it for you. That is precisely how people end up with teenagers they don't know, understand, or recognize.

Just in case you question our perspective on parenting matters, know that we have raised three social justice–minded kids. So far they have all stayed out of trouble, stayed on the honor roll, and been the envy of their peers' parents. We have failed plenty as parents, but we did not fail to teach them what we believe is important. They are free to form their own adult opinions in their own time, but when we release them into the wild, we know that they know what we value and believe. We know it's sinking in because our college-aged kiddo spent many years volunteering his time and talents tutoring kids and teaching coding in urban environments. Our middle child developed her own "Self-Care and Global Awareness" curriculum that she teaches to kids at a homeless shelter, and she formed a school club whose members find homeless people on the street of our city and just sit and talk with them. The youngest is only eight, but she is aware of the inequity in the world and we hope she follows her siblings' examples.

CALL TO ACTION

Get out and find new experiences, new challenges, and new friends.

Chapter Six

Assumptions are biases that can destroy relationships. Can you remember a time when someone made an assumption about you that wasn't true? Was it funny? Hurtful?

We all know what the kids say: "When you assume you make an ass of u and me." It is silly, of course. But as with many lessons learned in kindergarten, it is indeed useful. People do not often enjoy being pigeonholed, labeled, or thought of as one-dimensional. People are complex. Being human is hard. And the more marginalized or unfamiliar your group is, the more challenging it is to navigate the perils of everyone else's assumptions. Don't think of assumptions as harmless generalizations—see them for the biases they actually are.

Tiffany recalls a cycle of assumptions that followed her through her educational experiences.

I was often the only black student in a sea of white faces. My minority status was omnipresent and the norm for me. I actually didn't mind at all until the lessons on slavery or black history came up. Everyone would look at me and assume I was some sort of race expert, even as a child. Maybe they were looking for my reaction—who knows? But I was asked questions about being black and I did not like being put on the spot, as if that was my only identity. Then there was the inevitable arrival of another black student. If it was a boy, everyone assumed that I was going to date

him. Or at least they thought that I should date him—
because we were both black.

This is what our society does; it creates stereotypes and rein-forces them. The kids who made those assumptions probably did not have open conversations with their parents about race. If they did, then did their parents tell them that everyone should stick to their own kind? Not many families will go on record saying that, though some will. Parents who fail to talk to their kids about dif-ferences will end up with kids who pick up on societal stereotypes and run with them.

For me, the worst assumption by far was the one
teachers often made. As the daughter of a military
officer, I moved around a lot. I was a professional "new
kid." Again, I didn't actually mind. It was an adven-
ture. What got under my skin was the fact that most
every new teacher assumed I would be a low per-
former. How did I know? They didn't tell me, if that's
what you are thinking. Can you tell when someone
thinks less of you than others? The overt cues were that
I would be placed in the remedial groups first, or be
patronized in some irritating way. That attitude was
usually followed with visible shock and disbelief when
I proved to be a top performer, if not the *top performer*
in all of my classes. Someone had to be at the top of
the class. Why was it such a surprise that it was me?

Tiffany was able to recognize these blatant displays of unfair and unwarranted assumptions, but it isn't always so easy. Attribu-tional ambiguity is a concept that describes how hard it can be to determine why bad things are happening to you. It's an experience that plagues minorities and marginalized groups in particular.

Basically, it means that when you are a member of a marginalized group, you never know whether something happens to you because you are a member of that group or whether it just happened randomly. It is the source of great anxiety. Think about the phenomenon of "driving while black." Many African Americans and people of color will tell you that they are pulled over just for being minorities. Data support that fact, but could it also be speeding? A missing taillight? An expired tag? When you are in a minority group and bad things happen, sometimes it's because bad things happen. But as a result of our checkered human history, sometimes it's because of bias.

● **Learning to ask and not assume is a key skill to overcoming bias.**

Our assumptions get us into all kinds of trouble. Never assume that you know or understand another person's perspectives or experiences. Even if you have been through something very similar, or know someone who has, individual experiences are deeply personal and inherently unique. People take great offense when you think you know who they are without ever asking about their experience.

Our friend Marianne Vermeer shared a great example of what happens when we limit our perspective through assumptions.

There is a bumper sticker in places like Iowa and Michigan (where there are large populations of people who have immigrated from the Netherlands over the past century): "You're Not Much If You're Not Dutch." It pointedly reminds me that the Dutch have a bit of a superiority complex. Their country is managed well and the Dutch pride themselves on hard work, thrifty and fair management, and a belief that you support your own. Those who cannot find work that pays a living wage or don't know what a Calvinist work ethic is may deserve charity for a while but, the thinking goes, they really need to get their act together. Living and working in cultures where there are far fewer opportunities and a different approach to work brought home to me that my assumptions don't always hold water outside of the resource-rich midwestern US. Being in rural villages in Alaska as a college student amongst Native Americans whose culture and way of life reaches back centuries started me on a journey of looking at the world with less "Dutch eyes." Learning about the lives of Egyptians who lived on pennies a day because of a lack of education or a physical ailment made me realize that not all of us are born into circumstances that provide equal opportunity. Seeing the dignity with which these new friends lived their lives was humbling. I no longer have one of those bumper stickers.

One of the best ways to sidestep assumptions is simply to cultivate an essential skill: curiosity. When someone tells you they experienced racism, what's your response? What is your gut-level reaction? Is it, "I'm sure it wasn't racism. Joseph's not like that, he's a good guy!" Or, "Really? That's terrible. If you want to talk about it, I'm here for you." Developing the curiosity reflex goes a long way toward opening doors, extending empathy, and building connections. Interactions where you let your mental models invalidate others' experiences serve to close doors and fuel disconnection. So pay attention to what others are saying and your reactions. And when your opinions differ, assume for a moment the other person is right and ask them about their experiences and viewpoints. You don't have to agree to be friends, but slowing the rush to disagreement and judgment goes a long way.

In her excellent book *Why Are All the Black Kids Sitting Together in the Cafeteria*, Beverly Tatum talks about how this dynamic works with children. Little children naturally play together across all racial and cultural differences. They notice the difference, but for the most part they don't assign any meaning to them. Fast-forward to early high school. A black freshman, Seth, and white freshman, Jim, have been friends for years. They've been together since kindergarten, had sleepovers together, tried out for track and band. Early in the school year the English teacher, Mrs. Morris, asks her students to read passages from Dickens' *Great Expectations* aloud. After Seth finishes, she comments, "Well done, Seth. You're so articulate!"

Seth, taken aback, says to Jim at lunch, "Did you hear what Mrs. Morris just said? I think she's totally racist!"

At that moment, Jim has a choice: ask, don't assume, or the opposite, assume and don't ask.

What Dr. Tatum points out in her book is that most youth, and most adults, take the second path. And it looks something like this:

"Mrs. Morris isn't racist! She's really nice. She's always been really nice to me. I think you're misinterpreting what she said." Maybe he adds, "Don't be so sensitive, she gave you a compliment!" Jim's assumption is that his experience—Mrs. Morris has been nice to him—means that Seth's interpretation is invalid and must be wrong. Yet Jim, as a young white man, has not had conversations with his family about how to navigate race in America, he's never been given "the talk" that young black men receive, and his dinner table conversations are unlikely to be about how to navigate a biased society that is likely to assume he is less capable because he is white.

Seth, on the other hand, has grown up in an African American family with parents who came through the civil rights movement as children. They have memories of the South's massive resistance to desegregation. And so they teach their children to pay attention to how they're treated and to be wary of anyone who would discount their intellect or their gifts because of the color of their skin.

And so, with this gap in experience, a small statement begins to create a rift between friends who have very different lenses through which they see the world.

Meanwhile, Seth shares his experience with some of his black friends, who listen with empathy, and know how to ask good questions without assuming that he is wrong. And thus, the small step Jim makes in assuming his experience is right and Seth's is wrong leads to a small fissure that eventually ends in the black and white kids sitting separately in the cafeteria, surrounded by people who share their experiences and know how to talk about them.

But it doesn't have to go this way.

Jim could have said "Dude, that sucks!" or whatever kids say these days to indicate empathy. "But let me be honest, I don't really get it. Help me understand." By asking Seth to interpret his experience rather than assuming he understands already, Jim can build a bridge, not based on common experience, but rather based on common humanity that seeks to support others when they are hurting. Asking and suspending assumptions builds connections. Assumptions and judgment drive disconnection.

Our friend Andreas Addison has some interesting perspectives on how others' assumptions about him have made his work of reducing poverty in Richmond, Virginia, more difficult than it needs to be. As a white man working for city hall, people made assumptions about him that were neither true nor helpful.

As part of my job working in city hall in Richmond, Virginia, with a self-proclaimed title of Civic Innovation, I'm focused on bringing best practices and new ways of thinking to how cities operate and how government can work with and for the people.

One of my first projects I was tasked with was defining "who is the poverty population of Richmond?" It was really interesting looking at the racial makeup of poverty in Richmond. It's majority African American. And in that I was faced with a lot of racial undertones of just understanding who they are. People thought they knew what poverty was themselves, because they identified as African Americans, thus anything with the poor they could relate to because they themselves are black and they could say they knew what was going on. And I feel like that discredited me. And I remember facing that battle frequently, where it was, "I can't talk about poverty because I'm not black."

And it became an argument for myself, because I grew up poor. I grew up in a very rural part of Virginia where my parents were on food stamps for a while, my dad was unemployed, and we were really struggling to make ends meet month to month. I can relate to the struggles and challenges of being poor, but of course that was in a rural setting. I don't know what it's like being poor and African American in an urban setting, but I do know what it's like to be poor. And while I can't identify with the racial elements that create further separation, it doesn't mean I can't relate to it or I don't want to know how that works. I feel that that's what Richmond showed me.

I will never know what it's like to be poor AND black. That was one of the things I had to embrace. My experience is mine, but I also disagree with the fact that just because you're African American you know how to help those that are poor. I find that there's this battle with "who am I visibly and who am I internally?" I had to overcome my past, my parents, where I came from, but also because of who I am visibly, people automatically put me in a bucket.

This past year I worked on a health-care project with Code for America and the Richmond Health Department. One of the coolest parts about walking into the community resources center in Creighton Court and just being able to talk with anybody was knowing that I needed to dress down, be approachable, and have to actually initiate the conversation, saying, "I don't know what you're dealing with, but I want to learn, because I want to help." They want to hear that I hear what they're saying and there's a value to that. I came back once a month for eight months to show that I'm in this for the long haul. With that I think there's an approachability. I found that a lot of these people who live in these courts are huggers.

In an organizational context, the interrogative approach can be used to coach people and help them grow professionally and as individuals. Telling people what to do and assuming what they may think are both traps. People can easily resent an authority figure who purports to know it all. Asking open-ended, nonjudgmental questions empowers people to find their own solutions and to think critically. Executive coaches, teachers, and counselors use this technique to take people off the defensive and acknowledge the other person's value.

AVOID	Try Instead . . .
Questions with embedded **advice**: "Don't you think it would be a good idea to . . ." (Follow my advice!) "Maybe you should . . ." (You should!) "Just relax. Don't take the situation so seriously . . ."	Invite the participants to solve their own problems. "What solutions can you see to this situation?" "Have you been in situations like this before? How did you handle it then?"
Questions that **judge**: "Are you being as kind as you could be in this situation?" (Implied: you're not being kind enough!) "What would your parents think of your actions?" (Implied: your parents would disapprove!) "Is that a good idea?" (Implied: that's not a good idea!)	Validate the experiences and perspectives of others. Invite them to consider different perspectives: "I understand that this situation is difficult for you. Can you tell me more about that?"
Questions that **diagnose**: "Maybe what's actually going on is that you're angry because . . . ?" "Are you insecure because you . . . ?"	Asking people to describe how they're feeling and why: "I sense that you feel strongly about this subject. Can you tell me how you're feeling right now?" "It seems as though you're angry. Is that accurate?" "What about this situation stirs these emotions in you?"

Tiffany struggled with this concept until she sought executive coaching certification.

I am a person who wants to solve problems. I want to get to the root of an issue and fix it. Unfortunately, when dealing with people, one cannot assume that everyone wants to have their problems fixed. It has taken me a very long time to believe that some people just want to be heard, supported, and sometimes comforted. I used to assume that if someone shared a problem with me, they were tacitly asking for advice. Lots of people do come to me for advice, but I have had to learn the difference between a solicitation for advice and someone who just wants a sounding board. Becoming a certified professional coach was challenging. I had to let go of my long-held assumptions about human motivation. I used to be under the impression that executive coaches and counselors gave advice. Now I understand that we empower our clients to find solutions themselves. We can hold them accountable to their stated goals, reflect what we see back at them, and celebrate their victories. What we cannot do is tell them what to do or how to do it—no matter how obvious the solution may seem or how tempting the situation. Coaches have to get out of the way and let their clients do the work.

We had the pleasure of meeting two amazing researchers who developed a tool to help you understand why asking is important and to help you get more comfortable doing so. (Don't) Guess My Race was created by Michael Baran and Michael Handelman, cofounders of Interactive Diversity Solutions. Michael Baran, PhD, is a cultural anthropologist who has researched issues related to race and diversity for 20 years. He has taught courses on these subjects at Harvard University and the University of Michigan and consults for businesses and schools around race-related issues. Michael Handelman has been creating educational interactive multimedia for the past 14 years. He has produced and designed over 100 products with combined sales of over 50 million units. Several of these products have won awards such as the Educational Toy of the Year, Children's Technology Review All Star Award, and Parents' Choice Gold Seal.

Using this program can be effective because it is based on social science research that decreases implicit bias while increasing cultural understanding and empathy. Use it to actively disconfirm stereotypes as mentioned in the fourth condition of contact theory in chapter 2.

Activity #9 – Question Your Assumptions

Visit tmiconsultinginc.com and click the eLearning tab at

http://www.tmiconsultinginc.com/elearning

for a free demo of the *(Don't) Guess My Race* game. The app is available for mobile devices in your device's app store. Some of the outcomes of using the program include:

- ◆ Improves working relationships
- ◆ Stimulates productive discussions about difficult issues
- ◆ Develops critical thinking perspective on diversity issues
- ◆ Enhances insight into cultural construction of identity

Ask, don't assume. Simple in concept, difficult in real life. But with practice, this essential skill can stop bias dead in its tracks— by not even letting your bias come out of your mouth in the first place! And by showing genuine interest in others' experiences through well-crafted questions, you are well on your way to building an authentic relationship.

CALL TO ACTION

Question your beliefs and opinions. Why do you believe what you do? Take a moment to distinguish assumptions from facts and identify the origin of your assumptions.

Chapter Seven

Listen, don't judge

What happens after you ask? You listen. And listening, as simple as it sounds, is an essential but challenging skill to practice when interacting with people who have ideas that are different or conflicting to you. Studies have repeatedly shown that most of us are terrible at listening, at least when measured by asking people to recall what others have said. One seminal study indicated that most of us only recall about 25 percent of what we hear.[1]

Listening empathetically is the key to helping you move beyond your assumptions about another person's experiences and perspectives. We spend our lives attempting to justify our perspectives and choices, and when someone shares a story that challenges our own worldview, most of us stop listening and start creating a defense of our own opinions.

Imagine a world where everyone is free to live life their way without causing harm. You can be part of that world if you suspend judgment long enough to get to know people for who they really are instead of who you think they are.

Here is an example from Matthew's experience:

When I was in seminary in the early 2000s, the mainline Christian denominations were debating whether to bless same-sex marriages, or allow gay and lesbian clergy to be ordained. Most of the students and faculty at my school fell on the conservative end of the theological spectrum. And so it was something of a surprise to see, published in the student newspaper, an alumnus's article defending same-sex marriage from a Christian perspective. Many people were upset. They felt the "safe space" of their ideologically similar bubble had been compromised. And others went into debate mode, defending their position and attacking the other.

I made a different decision. I e-mailed the author and asked him out to lunch. The author of the article, Steve, told me that I was the only one that reached out to learn more. Others, including at least one faculty member, only communicated with him in order to challenge what he said.

Don't get me wrong—I love a good debate. And at the time I would have described myself as conservative on the issue of LGBT inclusion in the church. But I also realized this was an amazing opportunity to listen, without judgment, to a voice that I was not exposed to on a daily basis.

And so at lunch, I heard Steve's journey of reconciling his faith and his sexuality. I asked questions, seeking to understand and not judge. And I accepted his invitation to go to a church service with the group Integrity, an LGBT-friendly group within the Anglican Church of Canada. In the end, the possibilities of my in-group expanded to include those who I had been taught to exclude.

We've established that like attracts like, which is part of the larger challenge. Nonetheless, we have come to know many people with similar stories where listening without judgment transformed their relationships. Don Cowles, a former human resources leader at Reynolds Metals Company, shared this story of how listening without judgment was an essential part of transforming the culture of the company.

I was head of HR at Reynolds Metals Company, and we were getting all the human resource leaders together. The issue was that HR at Reynolds, and in the industry generally, we were basically the enforcers of the rules. "Carry out the big boss's wishes!" We were not perceived as partners; maybe we were the enemy. So in this culture of employee empowerment that Reynolds was trying to create, the big question was: Could the HR department become an ally and give up some of its control over the system?

In order to make this change, Don decided to invite the HR leaders to embark on a listening process—listening to outsiders, listening to other leaders, but most of all listening to each other.

We had customers come speak. We had people outside of the organization come speak and present their perspectives. But then we had a cultural anthropologist come—the notion was that people are living out a story in your corporation and it's embedded in your organization. It's just seen radically differently by different people.

So we created a history timeline and put it up on the wall. It covered some years before the oldest person in the room who would have picked up stories, and it went to the present. And the first exercise was to put down the cultural events across history that were part of your experience of that time. The next was to put down the corporate events and stories, including the economic cycles, the layoffs, the plant expansions, the latest HR buzzwords of the time. And finally your personal story under that—where it intersected with that.

We discovered that people had such radically different experiences driven principally by when they came to the company. I was in my 40s, and I was made the head of HR in the company and these other HR professionals were in their 50s and 60s. I was being asked to lead because I wasn't bound up in the past. And what I learned was how wounded many were with the change, that it was a rejection of all they had done for all these years.

Until you hear another person's narrative, you don't even know it exists. I had no idea of the other efforts under other leaders that had been tried and where the cynicism had come from, which in part was wisdom—but I couldn't see it because I hadn't had the experience. I had no way of knowing, and nor could others, until we learned to listen.

Don shared this crucial insight that is at the heart of listening as a means to building relationships:

Creating authentic relationships requires an act of courage from the get-go, and a certain humility that you don't know everything. It begins with an appreciation of your own incapacity to understand.

It is honestly difficult to communicate how essential listening without judgment is because most of us think of it as a basic skill we already do well. We often conduct active listening exercises in our workplace trainings. Participants regularly mention how rare it is for someone to focus exclusively on listening to what they have to say without other distractions. No cross talk, no checking the phone or Apple watch, no glancing at the clock or the computer screen. We are surrounded by distractions, and mostly unpracticed at the skill of tuning out the wider world in order to simply listen to another person.

Perhaps more destructive than distracted listening is our habit of listening to others with an ear for where we can interject our own stories and experiences. Although there is nothing wrong with having a conversation and finding commonalities, it is different than pure listening and contributes to our inability to recall what others have said. The moment you start thinking about what you want to say, you have stopped listening.

The general difficulty most of us have actively listening to others translates to an even greater challenge when we try to listen to those with whom we have some significant differences of opinions or life experiences. When someone shares an experience that is unfamiliar to us, or an interpretation of an experience that challenges our worldview, it becomes even harder to not interrupt, challenge, debate, or otherwise insert ourselves into the conversation. But if we are to build authentic relationships across difference, this is exactly what we must do. Because in order to uncover our blind spots, we must check our ego long enough to really hear someone else's perspectives.

Activity #10 – Listening Lunch

Alarmed at the political homogeneity of his social media circles, Matthew once invited one of his friends who represented a difference of political perspective out to lunch. His goal? Listen for understanding in order to ensure that he didn't begin to dehumanize people with different political leanings.

Your task: Find someone who pushes your buttons or whose ideas you just don't understand or agree with. Take that person out to lunch. Pay if you're able. Practice asking open-ended questions (see the chart in chapter 6) and then, simply, listen. Don't contradict, don't challenge, don't debate. If that's a challenge, rest assured we're only asking you to do this for one lunch. But notice your reactions, and inquire when and why it's challenging for you.

If the idea of a listening lunch feels too nerve wracking, just go out to a public place with lots of foot traffic and observe people. Watch and listen. Allow the total strangers to just exist. If an organic interaction occurs, don't discourage it. Be present. Talk and listen. Smile without being creepy. Look without staring. But mostly just listen without judgment. Notice how often you formulate opinions about total strangers, but don't judge yourself for doing so. We all do it. Again, it's human nature. So just get out there and notice what you notice without trying to assign too much meaning to it. We are more interested in you getting into the habit of noticing people's humanity as well as your own. Whenever you feel judgmental or biased, try to reconnect with humanity by being still and listening to the cacophony of voices and sounds people make in a coffee shop, a park, or a train station. Everyone has a story, and when you keep that in mind, it pushes your bias a little further out into the periphery.

CALL TO ACTION

Catch yourself in the act of judging and make a different choice. Are you judging something about a person that they can't control? Their appearance? Their background? Remember that the choice to judge says far more about us than the person being judged. Judgment is a habit that we have to break.

Conclusion

If you have read this far, then you know that we as individuals do indeed have the power to overcome bias. You also know that we all have bias and that it's completely normal. That said, what happens when a critical mass of thoughtful individuals actively addresses interpersonal bias? One would think that if enough of us made a change for the better, we would experience a seismic shift in cross-cultural relations. Some recent analysis of historical US census data seems to demonstrate the power of this claim as it reviewed racial housing segregation in American cities in the early twentieth century. A *Washington Post* article, "White flight began a lot earlier than we thought,"[1] summarized this research and came to this conclusion (emphasis added):

> *The suburbs we know today effectively didn't exist at the time [early twentieth century], so whites were leaving these neighborhoods for other neighborhoods in the city. That makes this earlier form of white flight even more striking; their new homes didn't necessarily have lower taxes or better school districts, factors that complicated the motivations of later generations of whites. **The accumulation of all those individual decisions is an important part of explaining why segregation took root** in places like Baltimore, Philadelphia and Chicago. . . .*

What happened, however, was that these individual choices became embedded in the institutions that were created in later decades, reinforcing racial segregation through redlining and federal lending programs, the GI Bill's unequal racial application, and many other policies. It becomes clear, then, that while individual actions have an enormous and measurable impact, over time systems are built up to the point that the collective actions of individuals may never be able to reach the tipping point of creating systemic change.

The problem with the tipping point for bias is that we have collectively created countless interconnected national and global systems that function because of, not in spite of, institutional bias. Institutional bias is partly responsible for the resistance some people exhibit when bias and privilege emerge in conversation. Why on earth would the people who benefit most from biased systems want to encourage change in favor of equity? Bias and equity have a public relations problem, much like the term "diversity."

As diversity practitioners, we fight an ongoing uphill battle against the negative stigma associated with diversity. People believe diversity is a dirty word, or that the implications of addressing diversity include adverse publicity, litigation, or creating a fear-based "politically correct" culture where everyone walks on eggshells. No one wants to poke the diversity bear. The status quo seems superior to openness, transparency, and authentic inclusion. The same is true of bias and equity, only when we consider these, people often worry that it is a zero-sum game. If everyone has equitable access to resources and opportunities, then *my* opportunities will be reduced. This is a very shortsighted approach for all of the reasons detailed in the previous chapters. Diversity has been consistently proven to be advantageous to systems. Companies with more diverse boards of directors outperform companies with homogeneous boards. The fear of equity and inclusion is unfounded. Once more of us have built authentic relationships across difference, we will have new insight and motivation into establishing unbiased systems that benefit everyone—not just folks like us.

● **What's next? Addressing bias in systems.**

Did you know that dropping one letter from your name on your résumé can get you more returned calls from employers? At least if that one letter makes your name sound more white. A widely circulated story chronicled the story of a man, José, who, frustrated with a lack of attention from prospective employers, changed his name to Joe but kept everything else on his résumé the same.[2] The callbacks came within a week.

The information in this book applies not only to individuals, but also on a larger scale to organizations, governments, and other institutions. Homogeneity stifles creativity. Practically speaking, *Overcoming Bias* also applies to the workplace. If leaders allow their bias to go unchecked, preferential treatment can fuel costly lawsuits when protected categories, like race or gender, are involved.

Organizations are in-groups, and they should be massively inclusive. The more diverse and inclusive they are, the more appealing they are to high-potential talent and diverse demographics. It's important to recognize that *leaders have the power to cultivate this inclusiveness by addressing bias within their organizations and institutions.* They must create space for the expansion of in-groups and for nurturing authentic relationships across difference. Leaders should ask themselves:

1. Who are my organization's current friends?

2. Do we have clear avenues for in-group expansion?

3. What in-groups dominate my organization?

Organizational leaders frequently ask us how to expand their networks and target markets. Here is what we suggest:

- Professional associations frequently have several minority equivalents. Find them and send employees to join, speak, and network. Better yet, go yourself.

- Expand the list of minority vendors your company sources for goods and services.

- Attend job fairs at community colleges and historically black colleges and universities (HBCUs).

- Join the minority chambers of commerce (Asian, Latino, African American).

- Sponsor events hosted by marginalized demographics (women's conferences, LGBT events, disability awareness campaigns).

- Ask how you can help these organizations meet their respective missions.

So where do we go from here? Now is when we open our eyes to all of the bias that exists and persists within the systems all around us. We have a moral imperative to understand the origins of institutional bias, how it has evolved or devolved, and how we can create stronger, better, less biased systems. Bias is a fractal concept; it operates from the smallest scale of the individual perspective, to one-on-one relationships, to family systems and organizational structures and on up through governments and global relations. Our next task is to reevaluate the system at every level and determine who among us has the influence and locus of control to effect systemic changes. We, the authors, argue that every single one of us has influence on the system. Now we need to find out how to use that influence to move everyone forward.

Activity Guide

Activity number	Activity name	Chapter	Brief description
1	Job Association	1	Identify occupational bias
2	Implicit Association Test	1	Identify interpersonal biases
3	Personalization	2	Identify hot buttons
4	Devil's Advocate	3	See both sides of an issue
5	Get Out of the Zone	3	Be in the minority
6	The Power of Privilege TEDx Talk	4	The power of privilege
7	Diversity Inventory	5	How diverse is your circle of trust?
8	Cultural Inventory	5	How broad are your cultural influences?
9	Question Your Assumptions	6	Play *(Don't) Guess My Race* demo on TMI website or download app
10	Listening Lunch	7	Lunch with someone whose perspectives you don't agree with—and listen

Notes

Chapter 1

1. Tom Bartlett, "The Trustworthiness of Beards," *Chronicle of Higher Education* blog, April 14, 2010, http://chronicle.com/blogs/percolator/the-trustworthiness-of-beards/22581.
2. Paul Verhaeghen, Shelley N. Aikman, and Ana E. Van Gulick, "Prime and Prejudice: Co-occurrence in the Culture as a Source of Automatic Stereotype Priming," *British Journal of Social Psychology* 50, no. 3 (2011): 501, doi: 10.1348/014466610X524254.

Chapter 2

1. A variety of interventions have been tried in experimental settings, but their long-term impact is still unknown. See Calvin K. Lai et al., "Reducing Implicit Racial Preferences: I. A Comparative Investigation of 17 Interventions," *Journal of Experimental Psychology: General* 143, no. 4 (2014): 1765–1785, http://dx.doi.org/10.1037/a0036260.
2. This analogy thanks to the TEDx Talk by Jay Smooth, accessed at http://tedxtalks.ted.com/video/TEDxHampshireCollege-Jay-Smooth.
3. Gordon W. Allport, *The Nature of Prejudice* (New York: Perseus Books, 1979).
4. Jayson Seaman, Jesse Beightol, Paul Shirilla, and Bart Crawford, "Contact Theory as a Framework for Experiential Activities as Diversity Education: An Exploratory Study," *Journal of Experiential Education* 32, no. 3 (2010): 207–225, doi: 10.1177/105382590903200303.

5. Jennifer Mohaupt, Mary van Soeren, Mary-Anne Andrusyszyn, Kathleen Macmillan, Sandra Devlin-Cop, and Scott Reeves, "Understanding Interprofessional Relationships by the Use of Contact Theory," *Journal of Interprofessional Care* 26, no. 5 (2012), 370–375.

6. Keith R. Ihlanfeldt and Benjamin P. Scafidi, "The Neighbourhood Contact Hypothesis: Evidence from the Multicity Study of Urban Inequality," *Urban Studies* 39, no. 4 (2002), 619–641, doi:10.1080/00420980220119499.

Chapter 3

1. David J. Kelly et. al., "Three-Month-Olds, but Not Newborns, Prefer Own-Race Faces," *Developmental Science* 8, no. 6 (2005), F31–F36, doi:10.1111/j.1467-7687.2005.0434a.x.

Chapter 4

1. Robert Ellsberg, ed., By Little and By Little: *The Selected Writings of Dorothy Day* (New York: Alfred A. Knopf, 1983), 109.

2. Dorothy Day, "Poverty and Pacifism," *Catholic Worker* (December 1944), accessed online at http://www.catholicworker.org/dorothyday/articles/223.pdf.

3. Diana Kwon, "Poverty Distrubs Children's Brain Development and Academic Performance," *Scientific American*, July 22, 2015, http://www.scientificamerican.com/article /poverty-disturbs-children-s-brain-development-and -academic-performance/.

Chapter 7

1. Rebecca Brent and Patricia Anderson, "Teaching Kids How to Listen," *Education Digest* 59, no. 5 (1994), 67–70 (summary reprint from 1993 article in *The Reading Teacher*).

Conclusion

1. Emily Badger, "'White Flight' Began a Lot Earlier Than We Think," *Washington Post*, March 17, 2016, https://www.washingtonpost.com/news/wonk/wp/2016/03/17/white-flight-began-a-lot-earlier-than-we-think/?postshare=5601458329672363&tid=ss_fb.

2. Chelsea Vail, "Jose vs. Joe: A Case of Resume Racism," Capital Ideas blog, September 4, 2014, http://www.chicagobooth.edu/capideas/blog/2014/september/jose-vs-joe-a-case-of-resume-racism.

Acknowledgments

To our children, Seth, Naomi, and Saba, for putting up with our insane schedules. To Christy Coleman, Art Espey, Linda Nash, and David Campt for their mentorship. To Carla Pratt Keyes and our Hope in the Cities family for their thoughtful partnership and guidance. To Bill Martin, Kelly Chopus, Meghan Gough, Kelli Parmley, and Jason Smith for being our biggest cheerleaders and community partners. And last but not least, the TMI Consulting family, especially Laura Swanson Bowser, for being the supportive backbone we needed to make this book a reality.

Index

A

ableism, 56
accountability
    for biased attitudes, 21
    to a higher standard, 27
    to stated goals, 98
activity guide, 113
    See also specific activities
Addison, Andreas, 94–96
Adichie, Chimamanda, 84
African Americans
    Addison's experience working
        with, 95–96
    "driving while black" experience
        of, 91
    friendship rifts of, 94
    in-group bias and, 39–40
    in-group expansion and, 76–77
Allport, Gordon, 31
AND1, 58–59
appendix syndrome. See self-
        evaluation
assumptions (assuming), 89–100
    activity for questioning, 99
    Addison's experience with, 94–96
    asking vs., 89–100
    challenging, 86
    consequences of, 91–92
    cycles of, 89–90
    defined, 89
    in-group bias and, 40
    integrated approach to, 96–99
    racial identity and, 84, 89–90,
        93–94
    societal stereotypes and, 90
    uncovering, 47, 49, 50, 69
    See also stereotypes
attributional ambiguity, 90–91
authentic relationships, building
    across differences, 2–6, 30, 34–35,
        85–86
    benefits to companies, 110–111
    challenges, 31, 37–38

contact theory and, 31–32
Cowle's insight into, 102–105
Get Out of the Zone, activity, 50
hallmarks, 4, 37
in-groups, out-groups, and, 38, 72
with people who think differently,
    72
prerequisites, 31
privilege and, 59, 61–62
requirements, 59
role in overcoming bias, 72
role of listening, 4, 104–105
Smith's experience with, 60–61
strategy, 100
in the workplace, 74

B

Baran, Michael, 98–99
beards, trustworthiness of men with,
    7, 11
belongingness, 73
bias
    addressing, in systems, 111–112
    blind spots created by, 13–14
    consequences of not overcoming,
        xii
    contact theory and, 30–32, 71–72
    controlling/conquering, 85
    cycle of, breaking, 22
    defined, 7
    encouraging, 27
    generational, 14–16
    influence on goals, intentions, 13
    in-group, 40
    institutional, 3, 110, 112
    interpersonal/intergroup, 8, 109
    looking out for, 37
    against Native Americans, 16,
        17–18
    negative, 17, 18
    origins of, 14
    personal, 9, 30
    pervasiveness of, 1, 18

Index

About the Authors

Tiffany Jana and Matthew Freeman are agents of change who met at work, fell in love, and started a company together. They are an interracial couple who pride themselves on practicing racial reconciliation every day. As a white male/black female married couple, they represent one of the least statistically common marital racial pairings in the United States. They are aware of that fact because the company they cofounded focuses on diversity and inclusion, and together they are breaking ground in the development of metrics for their industry. They live and breathe diversity and are conspicuously joyous about the life they share.

Tiffany followed her mother's lead into the world of diversity and culture change. Her mother paved the way by giving Tiffany access to life in Mexico and Germany, thereby granting her a unique connection and insight into foreign cultures. Tiffany is now fluent in Spanish and German, holds an MBA, and is a doctor of management in organizational leadership. When she is not orchestrating her company's growth, she is usually travelling the world with her husband and cofounder.

Matthew discovered diversity at a young age, but in a profound way, when he attended graduate school in Vancouver, Canada. He experienced "otherness" in a new way, and a paradigm shift in his worldview. He has been actively working to bring people and communities together across differences ever since.

Matthew is always willing to take risks if the results might yield an improvement to the status quo. He doesn't just think outside the box, he lives there. He was the cofounder of a community house in an underserved neighborhood and a mentor to at-risk youth.

Their company, TMI Consulting, is the first Certified Benefit (B) Corporation in the diversity and inclusion industry worldwide. Values-driven work is at the core of Tiffany and Matthew's business model. TMI is a for-profit business with a nonprofit mission. Part of the triple bottom-line economy, TMI maximizes profits without marginalizing people or the planet. Tiffany and Matthew are proud to be using the power of business as a force for good as part of the global B-Corp community of social enterprises.

Many of the exercises and the style of this book reflect their company's ethos and aspirational approach to very challenging work. Diversity work is fraught with tension, and these cofounders have developed a proprietary approach to quantifying, qualifying, and energizing a difficult subject. Tiffany and Matthew prefer focusing on why diversity is an asset rather than the traditional deficit-based approach. Whether delivering a keynote, a seminar, or a plenary session, Matthew and Tiffany's audiences inevitably enjoy quite a few laughs and a greater connection with the participants in the room.

Tiffany and Matthew are raising three children and two cats together. The oldest offspring is in college; the 17-year-old, 8-year-old, and kitties live at home. Together, Matthew and Tiffany have lived, worked in, and visited 48 states, 8 Canadian provinces, and 25 countries.

You can read more about them and their work at

tmiconsultinginc.com

Berrett–Koehler
Publishers

Berrett-Koehler is an independent publisher dedicated to an ambitious mission: *connecting people and ideas to create a world that works for all.*

We believe that to truly create a better world, action is needed at all levels—individual, organizational, and societal. At the individual level, our publications help people align their lives with their values and with their aspirations for a better world. At the organizational level, our publications promote progressive leadership and management practices, socially responsible approaches to business, and humane and effective organizations. At the societal level, our publications advance social and economic justice, shared prosperity, sustainability, and new solutions to national and global issues.

A major theme of our publications is "Opening Up New Space." Berrett-Koehler titles challenge conventional thinking, introduce new ideas, and foster positive change. Their common quest is changing the underlying beliefs, mindsets, institutions, and structures that keep generating the same cycles of problems, no matter who our leaders are or what improvement programs we adopt.

We strive to practice what we preach—to operate our publishing company in line with the ideas in our books. At the core of our approach is stewardship, which we define as a deep sense of responsibility to administer the company for the benefit of all of our "stakeholder" groups: authors, customers, employees, investors, service providers, and the communities and environment around us.

We are grateful to the thousands of readers, authors, and other friends of the company who consider themselves to be part of the "BK Community." We hope that you, too, will join us in our mission.

A BK Life Book

This book is part of our BK Life series. BK Life books change people's lives. They help individuals improve their lives in ways that are beneficial for the families, organizations, communities, nations, and world in which they live and work. To find out more, visit **www.bk-life.com**.

Berrett–Koehler
Publishers

Berrett-Koehler is an independent publisher dedicated to an ambitious mission: *connecting people and ideas to create a world that works for all*.

We believe that to truly create a better world, action is needed at all levels—individual, organizational, and societal. At the individual level, our publications help people align their lives with their values and with their aspirations for a better world. At the organizational level, our publications promote progressive leadership and management practices, socially responsible approaches to business, and humane and effective organizations. At the societal level, our publications advance social and economic justice, shared prosperity, sustainability, and new solutions to national and global issues.

A major theme of our publications is "Opening Up New Space." Berrett-Koehler titles challenge conventional thinking, introduce new ideas, and foster positive change. Their common quest is changing the underlying beliefs, mindsets, institutions, and structures that keep generating the same cycles of problems, no matter who our leaders are or what improvement programs we adopt.

We strive to practice what we preach—to operate our publishing company in line with the ideas in our books. At the core of our approach is stewardship, which we define as a deep sense of responsibility to administer the company for the benefit of all of our "stakeholder" groups: authors, customers, employees, investors, service providers, and the communities and environment around us.

We are grateful to the thousands of readers, authors, and other friends of the company who consider themselves to be part of the "BK Community." We hope that you, too, will join us in our mission.

A BK Life Book

This book is part of our BK Life series. BK Life books change people's lives. They help individuals improve their lives in ways that are beneficial for the families, organizations, communities, nations, and world in which they live and work. To find out more, visit **www.bk-life.com**.

MIX
Paper from
responsible sources
FSC® C011935